Beethoven

HIS LIFE & MUSIC

Jeremy Siepmann

sourcebooks
mediaFusion

An Imprint of Sourcebooks Inc.®
Naperville, Illinois

Copyright © 2006 by Jeremy Siepmann
Cover and internal design © 2006 by Sourcebooks, Inc.
Cover photo © Corbis
Title page picture: Beethoven holding the manuscript of the *Missa solemnis*, by
J.K. Stieler, 1819.
Sourcebooks and the colophon are registered trademarks of Sourcebooks, Inc.

Published by Sourcebooks MediaFusion, an imprint of Sourcebooks, Inc.
P.O. Box 4410, Naperville, Illinois 60567-4410
(630) 961-3900
Fax: (630) 961-2168
www.sourcebooks.com

Originally published in the UK by Naxos Books.

Library of Congress Cataloging-in-Publication Data

Siepmann, Jeremy.
  Beethoven : his life & music / Jeremy Siepmann.
    p. cm.
  "Originally published in the UK by Naxos Books, 2006"--ECIP data.
  Includes bibliographical references (p.   ) and index.
  1. Beethoven, Ludwig van, 1770-1827. 2.
Composers--Austria--Biography. I. Title.

ML410.B4S58 2006
780.92--dc22
[B]

                                                                    2006012972

                    Printed and bound in the United States of America.
                         BVG 10 9 8 7 6 5 4 3 2 1

Contents

iv	On CD One
v	On CD Two
vi	About the Website
vi	About the Life & Music Series
vi	About Sourcebooks MediaFusion
vii	Preface
ix	Prologue: Beethoven in his Time
1	Chapter 1: The Ascendancy
21	Interlude I: Beethoven and the Piano
31	Chapter 2: Crisis
46	Interlude II: Chamber Music (1): Mixed Families
53	Chapter 3: The Hero
64	Interlude III: Beethoven and the Human Voice
71	Chapter 4: The Immortal Beloved
89	Interlude IV: Beethoven and the Orchestra
99	Chapter 5: Kidnapped
119	Interlude V: Beethoven in the Theatre
125	Chapter 6: The Master
136	Interlude VI: Chamber Music (2): Strings Alone
143	Chapter 7: Finale
156	Epilogue: The Truly Immortal Beloved
165	The Eighteenth-Century Background
175	The Nineteenth-Century Foreground
179	Personalities
187	Selected Bibliography
188	Glossary
197	Annotations of CD Tracks
205	Index
209	Acknowledgments
210	About the Author

On CD 1

Piano Concerto No. 2 in B flat, Op. 19
[1] **Finale: Rondo. Molto allegro**   5:56
Stefan Vladar, piano; Capella Istropolitana; Barry Wordsworth 8.550121

Piano Trio in C minor, Op. 1 No. 3
[2] **Finale: Prestissimo**   5:45
Stuttgart Piano Trio   8.550947

Symphony No. 1 in C, Op. 21
[3] **Finale: Adagio—Allegro molto e vivace**   6:01
Nicolaus Esterházy Sinfonia; Béla Drahos   8.553474

Piano Sonata No. 8 in C minor, Op. 13 "Pathétique"
[4] **Movement 1: Grave—Allegro di molto e con brio**   8:28
Jenő Jandó, piano   8.550045

Symphony No. 3 in E flat, Op. 55 "Eroica"
[5] **Movement 2: Marcia funebre**   12:51
Nicolaus Esterházy Sinfonia; Béla Drahos   8.553475

Piano Sonata No. 23 in F minor, Op. 57 "Appassionata"
[6] **Finale: Allegro ma non troppo—Presto**   8:09
Jenő Jandó, piano   8.550045

Symphony No. 2 in D, Op. 36
[7] **Finale: Allegro molto**   6:36
Nicolaus Esterházy Sinfonia; Béla Drahos   8.553476

Fidelio, Op. 72
[8] **Act II, No. 14: Quartet "Er sterbe!"**   5:03
Inga Nielsen, Leonora; Gösta Winbergh, Florestan;
Alan Titus, Don Pizarro; Kurt Moll, Rocco;
Nicolaus Esterházy Sinfonia; Michael Halász   8.660070–71

"Razumovsky" String Quartet in E minor, Op. 59 No. 2
[9] **Movement 3: Allegretto**   7:30
Kodály Quartet   8.550562

Violin Concerto in D, Op. 61
[10] **Finale: Rondo**   11:14
Takako Nishizaki, violin;
Slovak Philharmonic Orchestra; Kenneth Jean   8.550149

TT 78:28

For more information on these tracks, see page 197.

On CD 2

Piano Concerto No. 4 in G, Op. 58
1 Movement 2: Andante con moto   5:37
Stefan Vladar, piano; Capella Istropolitana; Barry Wordsworth 8.550122

Symphony No. 5 in C minor, Op. 67
2 Finale: Allegro   8:36
Nicolaus Esterházy Sinfonia; Béla Drahos   8.553476

Piano Trio in B flat, Op. 97 "Archduke"
3 Movement 3: Andante cantabile ma pero con moto   12:02
Jenő Jandó, piano; Takako Nishizaki, violin; Csaba Onczay, cello 8.550442

Symphony No. 7 in A, Op. 92
4 Finale: Allegro con brio   8:50
Nicolaus Esterházy Sinfonia; Béla Drahos   8.553477

Mass in D, Op. 123 "Missa solemnis"
5 Gloria: "Quoniam tu solus sanctus"   6:33
Nashville Symphony Orchestra and Chorus;
Kenneth Schermerhorn   8.557060

Piano Sonata No. 32 in C minor, Op. 111
6 Movement 2: Arietta. Adagio molto, semplice e cantabile   16:28
Jenő Jandó, piano   8.550151

String Quartet in B flat, Op. 130
7 Movement 5: Cavatina. Adagio molto espressivo   6:13
Kodály Quartet   8.554593

Symphony No. 9 in D minor, Op. 125 "Choral"
8 Finale: Presto   13:41
Hasmik Papian, soprano; Ruxandra Donose, mezzo-soprano;
Manfred Fink, tenor; Claudio Otelli, bass-baritone;
Nicolaus Esterházy Sinfonia and Chorus; Béla Drahos   8.553478

                                                            TT 78:50

For more information on these tracks, see page 202.

Visit the dedicated website for *Beethoven: His Life & Music* and gain free access to the following:

- Many of the works in full that are featured in part on the CDs
- Works by some of Beethoven's contemporaries
- A timeline of Beethoven's life, set alongside contemporary events in arts, culture, and politics
- Special features on particular topics

To access this you will need:

- ISBN: 1843791110
- Password: Ludwig

About the Life & Music Series

The Life & Music series presents fully rounded, accessible portraits of composers through an ideal mix of media: words, pictures, and the music itself. With its extensive catalogue of classical recordings, its experience of the classical music world, its expertise in the use of the Internet, and its growing reputation for educational material, Naxos is ideally placed to provide richly illustrated and authoritative biographies of the great musical figures in the western tradition.

About Sourcebooks MediaFusion

Launched with the 1998 *New York Times* bestseller *We Interrupt This Broadcast* and formally founded in 2000, Sourcebooks MediaFusion is the nation's leading publisher of mixed-media books. This revolutionary imprint is dedicated to creating original content—be it audio, video, CD-ROM, or Web—that is fully integrated with the books we create. The result, we hope, is a new, richer, eye-opening, thrilling experience with books for our readers. Our experiential books have become both best-sellers and classics in their subjects, including poetry (*Poetry Speaks*), children's books (*Poetry Speaks to Children*), history (*We Shall Overcome*), sports (*And The Crowd Goes Wild*), the plays of William Shakespeare, and more. See what's new from us at www.sourcebooks.com.

Preface

The ideal medium for a musical biography has yet to be devised. One essential ingredient on the road to its discovery, however, is the audible presence of the music itself. Notated illustrations are no substitute for the real thing. Only a minority of music lovers today can read a score, much less hear it in their heads, without recourse to an instrument (generally a piano or guitar). To that extent, the invention of the CD has been a godsend to the musical author. Where writers on art and literature have long been able to quote in evidence, printing either the original text or pictorial reproductions, writers on music have had to rely on inadequate verbal description. Then along comes the CD, compact as described, which slips easily into the inside covers, and the problem is solved. In the present case, we have decided to include only whole works, movements, or self-contained sections, so that the CDs may be listened to not only in conjunction with the text but purely for pleasure. The hope is that text and music will be mutually nourishing, in whatever mixture.

The book is specifically addressed to a general audience and presumes no formal musical knowledge on the part of the reader. The ratio of biography to musical commentary favors the former by about two to one. Technical terms are explained in the Glossary. The music is not treated in a separate section of the book, as in the conventional life-and-works format, but rather in a sequence of "Interludes," alternating with the biographical chapters so that readers can, if they wish, opt for a continuous narrative and turn to the specifically musical discussions later on. These musical interludes, in any case, are not analytical. They amount to a generically organized survey of Beethoven's output and also include some biographical material. They can be read in any order, but they have been arranged in such a way as to grow naturally out of the narrative chapters that precede them (which are themselves not without musical commentary).

While avoiding the kind of imaginative scene-setting that blights so many biographies, I have attempted to give the book some of the immediacy of a novel by allowing its protagonists wherever possible to relate the story in their own words. These give a far richer and more fascinating portrait of both the characters and their time than any amount of subjective "interpretation." That said, interpretation is inevitable: the mere selection of quotations is necessarily an act of interpretation, before commentary even begins. So, in a more passive sense, are the reader's responses to them. There are no absolute truths in biography beyond simple factual accuracy. This book is conceived as no more than an introduction, but with any luck it will inspire a lifetime of further journeys into the life and work of a man believed by many to be the greatest composer who ever lived, and among the very greatest of men.

Prologue: Beethoven in His Time

The music of the Classical era, still in a relatively early phase at the time of Beethoven's birth in 1770, was based on notions of order, proportion, and grace. Beauty and symmetry of form were objects of worship in themselves and combined to create a Utopian image, an idealization of universal experience. In the Romantic age, thanks in no small part to Beethoven's influence, this was largely replaced by a cult of individual expression, the unfettered confession of powerful emotions and primal urges, the glorification of sensuality, a flirtation with the supernatural, an emphasis on spontaneity and improvisation, and the cultivation of extremes. Where a reverence for symmetry had characterized the Classical era, Romanticism delighted in asymmetry. Form was no longer seen as a receptacle but as a by-product of emotion, to be generated from within. While the great Romantic painters covered their canvases with grandiose landscapes, the great Romantic composers, starting with Beethoven and Weber (but anticipated by Haydn in his oratorio *The Seasons*), attempted similar representations in sound. Music took on an illustrative function to a degree never previously attempted, although "program music" (music that tells a story) had been around almost as long as music itself. In its cultivation and transformation of folksong (or that which was mistakenly perceived as folksong), music also became an agent of nationalism, one of the most powerful engines of the Romantic era. Although this played a relatively minor part in Beethoven's output, we find it reflected in some of the late works by his adoption of German rather than the traditional Italian terminology (including his brief flirtation with the German word "Hammerklavier" as a substitute for the Italian "pianoforte"), and in his preference for Mozart's German operas—notably *The Magic Flute*—over his Italian ones.

A further feature of the Romantic imagination was a taste for extravagance. Here, particularly where instrumental music is concerned, Beethoven was a trendsetter. His "Eroica," "Pastoral," and "Choral" symphonies expanded the scope and size of the symphony to hitherto unimagined degrees, while his "Hammerklavier" Sonata was over twice as long as a typical Classical sonata by Mozart or Haydn.

The ideals and consequences of the French Revolution were a source of alarm to the rulers of the crumbling Holy Roman Empire. As a consequence, Austria, with Vienna as its capital, became a bastion against French imperialism, and an efficient police state in which liberalism, both political and philosophical, was ruthlessly suppressed. But the Viennese, as Beethoven perceived, were not natural revolutionaries. Rather, they were noted for their political apathy and an almost decadent taste for pleasure. More troublesome to them than their homegrown overlords were the two occupations by the French in 1805 and 1809, the second of which, in particular, brought considerable hardship to the city in the form of monetary crises, critical food shortages, and a fleeing population, while Austria as a whole suffered serious political and territorial setbacks. With the final defeat of Napoleon in 1814, however, Austria recouped many of her losses, and during the Peace Congress of 1814–15 became the principal focal point of European diplomatic, commercial, and cultural activity. It was during this period, the capital now awash with visiting dignitaries and their entourages, that Beethoven's *Fidelio* was mounted twenty-one times with consistent success. But while the festivities associated with the Congress marked a return to gaiety, they could also be seen as a wake for an age whose time was over. Increasingly, throughout Europe, bankers, and businessmen replaced the nobility and landed aristocracy as the principal arbiters of taste and culture. To an altogether new extent, music passed out of the palaces and into the marketplace. Composers were decreasingly dependent on aristocratic patronage. They now relied for their livelihood on the sales of their work or, more commonly, on their income as teachers of the well-to-do—and those who aspired to be so. Vienna at that time (and it was not, even then, one of the larger cities) housed something in excess of 6,000 piano students. Performers, ever more reliant on the fickle patronage of a fee-paying public, emerged as a specialized breed of their own. Yet in the realm of the public concert, Vienna lagged well behind London. Although orchestral concerts had been mounted there since the 1770s, it was not until 1831, four years after Beethoven's death, that it acquired its own purpose-built concert hall. Throughout his life, concerts took place either in the palaces of the declining nobility, or in theatres (often privately owned and managed), or in ballrooms and other halls, none of them originally designed for music.

Inevitably, changes in social structure were accompanied by changes in taste. Especially after the hardships of the Napoleonic era, the public mood was for lightweight, escapist entertainment, most spectacularly exemplified by the new wave of lightweight Italian opera. This period marked the lowest ebb in Beethoven's fortunes as a composer, and the height of his anger and disgust at the society around him.

Beethoven's relationship to the politics of his time was as individual, and sometimes as contradictory, as he was himself, and was based on a deep-rooted sense of natural justice, a powerful if not very precisely defined belief in a moral élite, and a curiously naïve association of virtue with hard work and the overcoming of difficulties. "What is difficult is also beautiful, good, and great," he once wrote. In his own life he seems frequently to have created difficulties for their own sake, or at any rate as a prerequisite of moral nobility. In 1816 he wrote in his journal, "The chief characteristic of a distinguished man: endurance in adverse and harsh circumstances." Nobility was a matter of moral virtue, not heredity; but it did constitute an élite, and only those who had achieved it were fit to rule. That rulers were both necessary and desirable Beethoven never doubted, and he could never rid himself entirely of his admiration for Napoleon. While he championed the rights of humanity and saw it as a duty to give succor to the needy and the disadvantaged, he was by no means an apologist for the tenets of the French Revolution (the dominant political fact of European life in his youth). He publicly deplored the repressive actions of the Habsburg rulers in whose domain he had chosen to live, and admired the British for their form of parliamentary democracy, yet he was never wholly a democrat. He believed in a hierarchical, paternalistic society and generally scorned the proletarian masses, declaring flatly that "the common citizen should be excluded from higher men."

As regards his wider culture Beethoven was well read, especially considering that he had had no formal schooling after the age of eleven and his family environment contained little to encourage his literary interests. His lifelong love of poetry was nourished largely by his compatriots, notably Goethe, Schiller, Klopstock, and the lesser-known Wieland, Gleim, Amandus Müllner, and Friederich Werner. He was also a passionate devotee of Shakespeare and Homer, and a great enthusiast for the works of Ovid, Pliny, and (a guiding influence) Plutarch. He had a good working knowledge of the Bible, and in his later years became interested in a number of Oriental writers. Contemporary fiction seems to have occupied very little of his reading; though, again in later years, he took a fancy to the novels of Sir Walter Scott. Among philosophers, he was particularly drawn to Immanuel Kant. To judge from his letters and conversations, and from the evidence of his contemporaries, he would seem to have been largely indifferent to the visual arts.

To describe Beethoven as a transitional figure would be a misleading oversimplification. Yet in the realm of music he was *the* great bridge from the Classical to the Romantic era. Indeed, in many ways he was its architect. Through the singleminded pursuit of his artistic destiny, as he saw it, he changed the rules. To a degree unmatched by any other single figure, he transformed the role, character, and perception of the artist in society.

A striking feature of Romanticism was the cult of the hero, especially as represented in the writings and art of the ancient Greek and Roman civilizations. Given the character of his music (particularly that of his middle period) and the many entries and quotations in his journal concerning heroes and the heroic, there can be little doubt that Beethoven envisaged himself as a hero in the great Classical mold. Closely allied to the cult of the hero was the cult of the genius, which arose in the late eighteenth and early nineteenth centuries in reaction against the concept of the musician as an artisan—a servant rather than a master. Even Haydn had worn a uniform for most of his adult life, while Mozart had literally been kicked out of a room by an agent of his employer, the Prince-Archbishop of Salzburg. That the "genius" in Beethoven's case was both singular and eccentric only added to his appeal and served to fire his own imagination. Beethoven's unique development as a composer was at least in part a reflection of his time. History was ripe for his emergence.

Chapter 1

The Ascendancy

The Ascendancy

Music is the wine which incites us to new creation; and I am the Bacchus who presses this glorious wine for mankind, and grants them drunkenness of the spirit. When they are again sober, they will have fished up much which they may take with them onto dry land.

Ludwig van Beethoven

In all likelihood, the stocky, swarthy, tousled little man who made that statement was the first great composer to assume the identity of a god—albeit the god of wine. But modesty was never his game. He was probably also the first composer who consciously and repeatedly wrote for posterity. And why not? He kept good company. On another occasion he wrote:

I am well aware that God is nearer to me in my art than to others. I consort with Him without fear. I have always recognized and understood Him. Nor am I in the least anxious about the fate of my music. Its fate cannot be other than happy. Whoever succeeds in grasping it shall be absolved from all the misery that bows down other men.

This was quite a claim. Despite appearances, however, Beethoven was not being arrogant. He was talking about his own experience, as a survivor, and as a man who knew the difference between real joy and mere pleasure. In one way or another, most of the music he wrote proclaims that joy; yet much of it was the product of immeasurable suffering. Put at its most simplistic, his life can be seen as a heroic battle against adversity, in which defiance gave way to submission, and ultimately to a transcendent vision in which such attitudes seem all but irrelevant. In his music we may come as close as we can get to solving the ancient paradox of the irresistible force meeting an immovable object. Over a century and three quarters after his death, Beethoven remains the most titanic wrestler in musical history.

Beethoven's birthplace in Bonn

He was born in the smallish German Rhineland city of Bonn in 1769, 1770, and 1772 (it was characteristic of his singularity to have been born not once but thrice). The first Ludwig was indeed born in 1769, but, like so many children of that time, expired within a week. The second—of the same parentage—followed some twenty months later, born (probably) on December 16, 1770, and baptized (certainly) the following day; and the third never really existed, save in the lifelong confusion of Ludwig the second. Late in life he wrote to an old friend:

I am sure you will not refuse me a friendly request. I beg you to see to my certificate of baptism... If you yourself think it worth the trouble to hunt up the matter, and care to make the journey from Coblenz to Bonn, put everything down to my account; but there is one thing that you must bear in mind, namely, that a brother was born before me who was also called Ludwig, only with the additional name Maria, but he died. In order to fix my exact age, this must therefore be first found, for I already know that through others a mistake has been made in the matter, and that I have been regarded as older than I actually am. Unfortunately I have lived a long time without ever knowing my own age. I once had a family book, but it has gone astray, Heaven knows how! So do not be angry, if I commend this matter very warmly to you, to find out about Ludwig Maria and the present Ludwig who came after him. The sooner you send the certificate the more will I be in your debt.

It was neither the first nor the last time that he had asked this favor of a friend; and in each case he vigorously refuted the accuracy of the evidence when it was produced. If Beethoven himself had trouble with his age, others, including some who knew him, seem to have had trouble with his names–first, last, and middle. He was known variously as Ludwig, Louis, Luis, and Luigi, thereby embracing four nationalities, while his family name appears from time to time as Betthoven, Bethofen, even Bephoven, with "van" often being exchanged for "von" (the "van" is Dutch in origin, and carries none of the aristocratic clout of the German "von"). There was in fact a fourth Ludwig van Beethoven, the composer's grandfather–a greatly respected Kapellmeister who served in many ways as the young Beethoven's role model. This the father was emphatically not.

Johann Beethoven, a heavy-drinking court musician (he sang tenor and taught singing and piano), saw in his obviously talented son the chance of worldly salvation for himself, and ruthlessly set about trying to produce a second Mozart. From the beginning, Beethoven paid heavily for his father's ambitions. More than one visitor to the house saw the little boy weeping as he practiced. Repeatedly, he was locked in the cellar and/or deprived of food. Returning from the tavern after midnight, the drunken Johann would frequently shake the sleeping child awake and force him to the piano, where he was made to practice until dawn. This, at least, is the story that has been told, in reputable biographies, through the better part of two centuries. Much may be true; but the fact is that there are no reliable documentary sources to corroborate most of it. As a teacher and mentor, Johann was no Leopold Mozart, and Ludwig, while conspicuously gifted, was no Wolfgang Amadeus—though he became an excellent pianist for his age, and a creditable violinist.

When Ludwig was eight (though billed as six), his father arranged a concert in Cologne as a showcase for his son and another pupil, the contralto Johanna Averdonk. It was a damp squib, of which not a single account, either private or public, survives. Whatever retribution may have been visited upon the son (this, too, is unrecorded), the concert's evident failure was a damning indictment of the father's teaching, which in any case had been effectively confined to instrumental training. Every sign of the boy's earliest urges to compose, from his very first improvisations, had met with angry scoldings or actual punishment for disobedience. Even in childhood, however, the stubbornness and resilience so widely remarked in Beethoven's maturity were deeply entrenched. In the course of the next five years, he had lessons in harpsichord, piano, violin, viola, organ, and horn from a motley collection of local teachers. Not until 1781 did he receive any sustained, systematic tuition in composition. This

> Returning from the tavern after midnight, the drunken Johann would frequently shake the sleeping child awake and force him to the piano.

was provided by Christian Gottlob Neefe, a relatively recent arrival in Bonn's musical establishment who also became Beethoven's sole keyboard teacher.

The first public notice of the boy's talent and achievements appeared two years later, in a letter to Cramer's *Magazin der Musik*:

> *Louis van Betthoven [is] a boy of eleven years and of most promising talent. He plays the clavier very skillfully and with power, reads at sight very well, and—to put it in a nutshell—he plays chiefly* The Well-Tempered Clavichord *[sic] of Sebastian Bach, which Herr Neefe put into his hands. Whoever knows this collection of preludes and fugues in all the keys—which might almost be called the* non plus ultra *of our art—will know what this means. So far as his duties permitted, Herr Neefe has also given him instruction in thorough-bass. He is now training him in composition, and for his encouragement has had [the boy's] nine variations for the pianoforte on a march by Ernst Christoph Dressler engraved at Mannheim. This youthful genius is deserving of help to enable him to travel. He would surely become a second Wolfgang Amadeus Mozart were he to continue as he has begun!*

Again we find the comparison with Mozart, and again the (surely innocent) mistake in Beethoven's given age. As it turns out, the author of the letter was Neefe himself.

On one point, all of Beethoven's teachers were agreed: he was not an easy pupil. Even in childhood, his attitude to tradition was something quite new in music, and it was later to change the course of history. With all the ruthlessness of genius, he took from the legacy of his elders only what made sense to him in terms of his own inner experience. The rest he discarded. In giving him *The Well-Tempered Clavier*, Neefe may have done more for Beethoven's future development than the rest of his teachers put together. Interestingly, Haydn and

Mozart, in Vienna, were discovering Bach at the same time, courtesy of the scholarly Baron van Swieten (who was to become the dedicatee of Beethoven's First Symphony). Astonishingly, *The Well-Tempered Clavier*, like most of Bach's works, remained unpublished some forty years after its completion and was circulated in manuscript copies alone.

> Beethoven asked Mozart to give him a theme on which to improvise. Mozart obliged and Beethoven did what he did best. Mozart was instantly riveted.

Except for a brief visit to Holland occasioned by the death of a relative, Neefe's recommendation of travel went unheeded for another four years. In the meantime, Beethoven progressed quickly. Within a year he was reliably deputizing for Neefe as court organist and was admitted to the Elector's court orchestra as assistant harpsichordist. In 1784, not yet fourteen, he was appointed second organist. By the time he turned sixteen, the Elector was sufficiently impressed by his accomplishments to subsidize a trip to Vienna for purposes of study with Mozart (who was then thirty-one, and engrossed in the composition of *Don Giovanni*). On first hearing him, Mozart allegedly reacted rather coolly. Beethoven, unperturbed, asked Mozart to give him a theme on which to improvise. Mozart obliged and Beethoven did what he did best. Mozart's attention was instantly riveted. Listening with increasing wonder, he tiptoed to the doorway of an adjoining room where some friends were sitting. "Keep your eyes on this one," he whispered. "Someday he will give the world something to talk about." So runs the much-repeated anecdote, although there are no eyewitness reports to substantiate it. Even if there were, however, eyewitness accounts are not necessarily more reliable than anecdote. From his friend and pupil Ferdinand Ries, for example, we hear that Beethoven greatly regretted never having heard Mozart play. From his friend and pupil Czerny, on the other hand, we hear that he heard Mozart repeatedly.

Beethoven playing at Mozart's home in 1787

Had Beethoven's hoped-for lessons with Mozart come to pass, we would undoubtedly know more. As it was, within a fortnight of his arrival in Vienna, Beethoven learned that his mother was seriously ill. She lived on for another three months before succumbing to tuberculosis at the age of forty. With his father sinking ever deeper into alcoholism, Beethoven, at sixteen, now took over full responsibility for the family: his father, two younger brothers named Carl and Johann, and an infant sister who died before the year was out. On September 15, 1787, he wrote to a recent acquaintance, Josef Schaden:

Well born, especially worthy friend!

I can easily imagine what you must think of me, and I cannot deny that you have good grounds for not thinking favorably of me. I shall not, however, attempt to justify myself, until I have explained to you the reasons why I hope my apologies will be accepted. I must tell you that from the time I left Augsburg my cheerfulness as well as my health began to decline. The nearer I came to my native city the more frequent were the letters from my father urging me to travel with all possible speed, as my mother was not in a favorable state of health. I therefore hurried forward as fast as I could, although far from well myself. My longing once more to see my dying mother overcame every obstacle and assisted me in surmounting the greatest difficulties. I found her still alive but in the most deplorable state; her disease was consumption, and about seven weeks ago, after much pain and suffering, she died. She was such a kind, loving mother to me, and my best friend. Ah, who was happier than I when I could still utter the sweet name, mother, and it was heard? And to whom can I say it now? Only to the silent images of her evoked by the power of the imagination. I have passed very few pleasant hours since my arrival here, having during the whole time been suffering from asthma, which may, I fear, eventually develop into consumption. To this is added melancholy, almost as great an evil as my malady itself. Imagine yourself in my place, and then I shall hope to receive your forgiveness for my long silence. You showed me extreme kindness and friendship by lending me money in Augsburg, but I must entreat your indulgence for a time. My journey cost me a great deal, and I have not the smallest hopes of earning anything here. Fate is not propitious to me here in Bonn. Pardon my detaining you so long with my chatter; it was necessary for my justification. I do entreat you not to deprive me of your valuable friendship; I wish nothing so much as in some degree to become worthy of your regard.

I am, with the greatest respect,
Your most obedient servant and friend,

L.v. Beethoven,

Court Organist to the Elector of Cologne.

Frau Beethoven had been a much-respected woman. She was a model of long-suffering virtue, but warmth was not her style. Few could claim ever to have seen her laugh; and she had not lavished any obvious affection on her eldest son. Yet it was to her influence that he (obliquely) attributed the code of ethics that he was at pains to emphasize throughout his life, always citing its origin in his childhood: "Since I was a child my greatest happiness and pleasure have been to do something for others;" "Since childhood, my zeal to serve our poor, suffering humanity in any way whatsoever has made no compromise with any lower motive;" "*Never, never* will you find me dishonorable!" etc. How he squared this with selling the *Missa solemnis* to several different publishers at the same time is a matter he never addressed in words. But this is to anticipate.

After a period of genuine poverty, bad health, and bouts of depression, Beethoven began in earnest to discover his powers. He made new friends—including the first in a long line of influential noblemen, Count Waldstein—and established himself as a virtuoso pianist without rivals. It was only a matter of time before news of his prowess spread well beyond the confines of Bonn and its environs. In 1791, Carl Ludwig Junker, who heard him at Mergentheim during a visit by the Elector's court orchestra, extolled his virtues in a letter to the *Musikalische Correspondenz:*

I heard also one of the greatest of pianists—the dear, good Bethofen, some of whose compositions appeared in the Speiers' Blumenlese in 1783, written in his eleventh year. True, he did not perform in public, probably the instrument here was not to his liking. But, what was infinitely preferable to me, I heard him extemporize in private. I was even invited to propose a theme for him to vary. The greatness of this amiable, lighthearted man as a virtuoso may be safely estimated from his almost inexhaustible wealth of ideas, the altogether characteristic style

of expression in his playing, and the great execution which he displays.
I know, therefore, no single thing which he lacks that is conducive to
artistic greatness. I have often heard Vogler upon the pianoforte, and
never failed to wonder at his astonishing execution; but Bethofen, in
addition to the execution, has greater clarity and weight of idea, and
more expression—in short, he appeals more to the heart, and is therefore
equally great as an adagio *or* allegro *player. Even the members of this*
remarkable orchestra are, without exception, his admirers, and all ears
when he plays. Yet he is exceedingly modest and free from all preten-
sion. He acknowledged to me, however, that on the journeys which the
Elector had enabled him to make he had seldom found in the playing
of the most distinguished virtuosos that excellence which he felt he had
a right to expect. His style of treating his instrument is so different from
that usually adopted that you feel he has attained the heights of excel-
lence through a path of his own discovery.

This "amiable, lighthearted man," so "exceedingly modest,"
was not quite yet twenty-one. Almost exactly a year later, he
left Bonn to take up permanent residence in Vienna. Junker's
rosy-eyed characterization would soon be outdated.

To be a pianist without rivals in Bonn was one thing; to be
such in Vienna was quite another. When Beethoven arrived
there in the second week of November 1792, the city housed
more than 300 professional pianists and upwards of 6,000
piano students. Beethoven was determined to vanquish them
all, and did nothing to conceal the fact. He had a powerful
competitive streak, and he entered, or in some cases actually
engineered, a series of pianistic duels in which he toppled
Vienna's pianists from their perches, one after another. Among
these was Josef Gelinek, who scarcely knew what had hit him:

Satan himself must be hidden in that young man! I have never in my
life heard anyone play like that! He improvised on a theme which I

gave him as I never heard even Mozart do. Then he played some of his own compositions which are in the highest degree remarkable and magnificent. He overcomes all difficulties and draws effects from the piano such as the rest of us couldn't even allow ourselves to dream about.

Another virtuoso, Daniel Steibelt, was so mortified by his pianistic trouncing at Beethoven's hands that he fled the room before Beethoven had finished and subsequently refused to attend any gathering at which Beethoven might also be present.

As noted by Junker, Beethoven's playing was something new; and it inspired a new kind of criticism, a new kind of experience for the listener. Even Mozart, who had died less than a year before Beethoven's arrival in Vienna, would never have prompted prose like this:

When once he began to revel in the infinite world of tones, he was transported also above all earthly things; his spirit had burst all restricting bonds, shaken off the yokes of servitude, and soared triumphantly and jubilantly into the luminous spaces of the higher ether. Now his playing tore along like a wildly foaming cataract, and the conjurer constrained his instrument to an utterance so forceful that the stoutest structure was scarcely able to withstand it; and anon he sank down, exhausted, exhaling gentle plaints, dissolving in melancholy. Again the spirit would soar aloft, triumphing over transitory terrestrial sufferings, turn its glance upward in reverent sounds and find rest and comfort on the innocent bosom of holy nature. But who shall sound the depths of the sea? It was the mystical Sanskrit language whose hieroglyphs can be read only by the initiated.

So wrote the composer Ignaz von Seyfried on Beethoven's "duel" with his closest Viennese rival, the much-esteemed Joseph Wölfl.

A letter to the *Allgemeine musikalische Zeitung* from another eyewitness gives a more dispassionate account that helps enrich the picture:

> *I shall try to set forth the peculiarities of each without taking part in the controversy. Beethoven's playing is extremely brilliant but has less delicacy, and occasionally he is guilty of indistinctness. He shows himself to the greatest advantage in improvisation, and here, indeed, it is most extraordinary with what lightness and yet firmness in the succession of ideas Beethoven not only varies a theme given him on the spur of the moment by figuration (with which many a virtuoso makes his fortune) but really develops it. Since the death of Mozart, who in this respect is for me still the* non plus ultra, *I have never enjoyed this kind of pleasure in the degree to which Beethoven provides it.*

After a highly respectful discussion of Wölfl's playing, he observes that "Wölfl enjoys an advantage because of his amiable bearing, contrasted with the somewhat haughty pose of Beethoven."

Carl Czerny, later one of Beethoven's pupils and a great connoisseur of piano playing, was much struck by the contrast between Beethoven's playing and Mozart's:

> *Mozart favored clear and markedly brilliant playing, based more on* staccato *than* legato, *and with a witty and lively execution. The pedal was seldom used and never necessary. The outstanding feature of Beethoven's playing, on the other hand, was a characteristic and passionate strength, alternating with all the charms of a smooth* cantabile. *He drew entirely new and daring sounds from the piano, partly by his use of the pedal, but also through the strict* legato *of his chords, which created a new type of singing tone and many other previously unimagined effects. His playing was spirited, grandiose and, especially in* adagio, *full of romantic feeling. His performances, like*

his compositions, were tone-paintings of a very high order and conceived only for a total effect.

As often as not, the effect was emotional dynamite. This was particularly true when Beethoven improvised:

In whatever company he might chance to be, he knew how to achieve such an effect upon every listener, that frequently not an eye remained dry, while many would break out into loud sobbing, for there was something wonderful in his expression, in addition to the beauty and originality of his ideas and his spirited style of rendering them. After ending an improvisation of this kind, he would often burst into loud laughter and mock his hearers on the emotion he had caused in them: "You are all fools!" he would cry. "Who can live amongst such spoiled children?"

At no time in his life was Beethoven an easy man. He was certainly no diplomat. And in his passion and exuberance he could be as thoughtless of his pianos as he often was of his friends. One of these was the composer Antonín Reicha:

Beethoven once asked me to turn pages for him. But I was mostly occupied in wrenching the strings of the piano which snapped, while the hammers stuck among the broken strings. Beethoven insisted on playing to the end, so back and forth I leapt, jerking out a string here, disentangling a hammer there, turning a page... I worked harder than he did!

Beethoven was much more, even in these early days, than just a pianist and piano composer. He had written two imposing cantatas, and a good deal of chamber music in which the piano plays no part. In 1795, now twenty-four, he was commissioned to write the dances for the annual charity ball at the famous

Beethoven's Broadwood piano

Redoutensaal. Surprising to many, now as then, is the curious fact that he found it far easier to write such music than to dance to it. In the ballroom, he was a liability.

Dancing in Vienna, more than in any other city in the world, was almost an obsession in those days. Indeed it was one of the things that helped to perpetuate the city's reputation as a citadel of genteel (and sometimes not so genteel) frivolity. Ballrooms and dance halls were almost as common as the numerous cafés, taverns, and beer halls. They were frequented by members of every class, often wearing masks to disguise their identity, because, as one upright historian proclaimed, "Many of these establishments, notwithstanding their decorous exteriors, are plainly institutions for more infamous purposes." Prostitution was rife at every level, something which the young Beethoven deplored. Entertainments, on the streets and in the theatres, were dominated by jugglers, puppeteers, rope-dancers, acrobats, and so on. The prevailing taste was for trivia rather than substance, escapism rather than philosophy, pleasure rather than education. But if there was escapism, there was also much to escape from. Beneath the surface of gaiety lay the workings of a ruthless police state. Dissidents were commonly arrested, flogged, and imprisoned, while hundreds of government spies had infiltrated almost every level of society.

Beethoven had few illusions about the society into which he had moved. In the summer of 1794 he wrote to a friend in Bonn:

> *We are having very hot weather here; and the Viennese are afraid that soon they will not be able to get any more ice cream. As the winter was so mild, ice is now scarce. Here various important people have been locked up; it is said that a revolution is about to break out—but I believe that so long as an Austrian can get his brown ale and his little sausages, he is not likely to revolt. People say that the gates leading to the suburbs are to be closed at 10 in the evening. The soldiers have loaded their muskets and you dare not raise your voice here or the police will take you into custody.*

In time to come, Beethoven himself would raise his voice, but for the moment he kept silent. He was not afraid, but felt broadly content with the situation as it was. He had no fundamental quarrel with the nobility, who were his most valuable patrons, both present and prospective; and what he valued at least as much as his career was the sense of belonging. In many ways, the noble and aristocratic families who welcomed him gave him a sense of comfort and security, and of being valued for himself, which he had rarely felt within his own family. There was also a curious, unspoken alliance between the repressive authorities and the broader world of culture. As in many despotic regimes, the police appreciated the pacifying effect that the arts could have, and the theatres most of all.

Improbable as it may seem, it was the police who prevented the closure of one of Vienna's principal theatres. To quote from their official memorandum: "The people are accustomed to theatrical shows. In times like these, when the character of individuals is affected by so many sufferings, the police are more than ever obliged to cooperate in the diversion of the citizens by moral means. The most dangerous hours of the day are the evening hours. These cannot be filled more innocently than in the theatre"—unless it was in the home, playing music with friends. Here, even more than in the ballroom, Beethoven was ready and willing to provide the wherewithal. Far more interesting and engaging than his dance music is some of the chamber music that he wrote for wind instruments, and for wind and strings combined. This, too, was entertainment; but here there was real musical conversation, with musical ideas taken up, exchanged, and developed, all with a masterly deployment of instrumental tone color.

Beethoven experienced much of his early Viennese life as a kind of liberation. Whereas in Bonn, as the unofficial head of the family, he had had in many ways to subordinate his own life to the needs of others, in Vienna he could savor the fruits of a kind of enlightened self-centeredness. Now he could put himself first; and his prime duty was to fulfill what he increasingly accepted as his destiny. It helped, of course, that despite his somewhat coarse exterior and his provincial manners, he had rapidly become the darling of the aristocracy—the wielders of power. He was indeed the talk of the town, first as a pianist, then, increasingly, as a composer. But he was well aware that all this had the potential to corrupt him as an artist. In his journal he would urge himself not to be deflected from what he now began to refer to as his "divine art":

> Now he could put himself first; and his prime duty was to fulfill what he increasingly accepted as his destiny.

Courage! In spite of all bodily weaknesses my spirit shall rule... This year must determine the complete man. Nothing must remain undone.

This meant admitting, at least in theory, that in spite of his genius, which he freely acknowledged, there were aspects of his craft which he still needed to learn. In the earliest phases of his Viennese life, Beethoven seems to have had lessons from practically everyone, if only to demonstrate how little he needed them. One of these, the esteemed pedagogue Johann Georg Albrechtsberger, is most memorable today for his magnificent verdict on Beethoven's future.

"If I were you, I shouldn't have anything to do with him. He has learned nothing and will never amount to anything."

Writing to a colleague, he warned, "If I were you, I shouldn't have anything to do with him. He has learned nothing and will never amount to anything." The most notable of Beethoven's teachers at this point was none other than the greatest and most famous composer in the world, Joseph Haydn. "From him," Beethoven once declared, "I learned absolutely nothing." His music, however, tells a different story.

Before God, Beethoven was genuinely humble. He was, in fact, genuine to a fault in everything he did or felt. For humanity, with its suffering and resilience, he felt a passionate if largely symbolic love. But for the generality of man, represented from an early age by his father, he felt on the whole a contempt that he did little to conceal. "The devil take you!" he once wrote. "Don't talk to me about your ethics and your moralizing. Power. Power is the morality of men who stand above the rest. It is also mine." Elsewhere, referring to men who thought of themselves as his intimate friends, he said: "I consider them mere instruments, on which I play when it pleases me. I value them accordingly as they are useful to me." Yet in his dizzying rise to the pinnacles of artistic power and social prestige, he really did appear to delight in the company of his friends, as they did in his. By all accounts, he relished conversation and laughter whether in taverns or in palaces, and he discovered that, against the odds, he was intensely attractive to women.

Beethoven's charms, however, like his sense of etiquette, were not always instantly obvious—as a pianist acquaintance of the Lichnowsky family, Frau von Bernhard, later recalled:

> *Whenever he came to visit, he used to stick his head in the doorway and make sure that there was no one there whom he disliked. He was small and very plain-looking, with an ugly red, pock-marked face. His hair was dark and hung shaggily around his face. His clothes were commonplace in the extreme. Moreover, he spoke in a strong dialect and in a rather common manner. In general, his whole being did not give the impression of any particular cultivation; in fact, he was unmannerly in both gesture and demeanor. He was also very haughty. I myself have seen the mother of Prince Lichnowsky, Countess Thun, going down on her knees to him as he lolled on the sofa, and begging him to play something. But Beethoven continued stubbornly to refuse.*

An elderly Countess on her knees before an uncouth pianoplayer in his twenties—and a Countess, moreover, who had been a patron of Mozart, Haydn, and Gluck! Another noble, her son Prince Lichnowsky, gave his household staff strict instructions that if ever he and Beethoven should arrive at the door together it was Beethoven who should be attended to first.

Beethoven's almost wholesale adoption by the nobility of Vienna was something as new as his music. Haydn, by contrast, now in his early sixties, had only recently discarded the servant's livery that he had worn for decades in the service of the Esterházy family. That Beethoven had real charm and could be delightful company is amply documented. When it came to observing the trappings of nobility, however, he showed, as we have seen, an almost aggressive disdain. As Ferdinand Ries observed:

> *Etiquette and all that goes with it was something Beethoven never learned or wanted to learn; thus his behavior often caused great embarrassment to the suite of the Archduke Rudolph when Beethoven first attended him. They attempted to force him to learn the formalities he was expected to observe, but he found this insupportable. He did, at one time, promise to improve in this—but that was as far as it went. The Archduke gave orders that Beethoven should be allowed to go his own way without hindrance. That, he explained, was simply the way he was.*

From the outset of his relations with the Viennese nobility, Beethoven insisted, not by stating as much but simply through his behavior, that he be treated on equal terms. As he later observed to one of his several royal patrons, "Prince? Of princes there have been and will be thousands. Of Beethovens there is only one." And the princes knew it. Almost from the moment of his arrival in Vienna he had been embraced and celebrated by the highest in the land. They were as much impressed by his nobility of spirit as he himself was. They reveled in his genius, and delighted in his exuberant self-confidence. And given his obviously incorruptible integrity, and his almost superhuman ability to manipulate the feelings of his listeners, many must actually have felt flattered by his attentions.

"Prince? Of princes there have been and will be thousands. Of Beethovens there is only one."

This would hardly have been so had it not been for his irreverent sense of humor. They loved his jokes. They loved the fact that he was so utterly unfazed by their rank. They loved his power. For all his lack of social graces, his gift for friendship paid dividends at almost every level. Indeed, the Beethoven of these early Viennese years seems, for the first time in his life, to have been almost intemperately happy.

Interlude I:
Beethoven and the Piano

Introduction

Beethoven transformed almost every medium he touched, and his minor works are relatively few. Even in his earliest published works, composed when he still identified strongly with the Classical movement exemplified by Mozart and Haydn, he expanded both the length and the emotional scope of received forms. The three piano trios of **Op. 1** and the three piano sonatas of Op. 2, all completed in 1794–5, are far longer than the average sonatas and trios of Mozart and Haydn. As a whole, Beethoven's piano sonatas require a level of virtuosity far beyond even the most difficult Haydn or Mozart sonatas, with the sole exception of Haydn's great Sonata No. 62 in E flat. While the average symphony by Haydn and Mozart lasts well under half an hour, Beethoven's **Third** and Sixth symphonies run to nearly fifty minutes, while the **Ninth** lasts around seventy. In matters of form, as in so much else, Beethoven established his independence early on and drew on tradition only as it suited him. He uses Classical "sonata form" with even greater freedom and individuality than his teacher Haydn. The powerfully integrated structures of Beethoven's music (which generations of music lovers have sensed without

CD 1
track 2
www.naxos.com

CD 1
track 5
www.naxos.com

CD 2
track 8
www.naxos.com

any need of technical knowledge) derive to a large extent from the organic nature of their development. This is not something one needs to be aware of when listening. It is quite possible that Beethoven himself was unaware of it. But the degree of thematic unity in his works is remarkable. Almost all the themes in his famous **"Pathétique" Sonata**, for instance, derive in one way or another from the pattern of the first four notes, while the second main theme in the first movement of the **"Appassionata" Sonata** is basically a variant of the first, turned upside down—a Haydnesque technique used with unprecedented expressive force.

Few composers before Beethoven even approach the range, intensity, and dramatic opposition of emotions that is evident in all of his great works, and many of his minor ones. And no composer approached his violence. It is hardly an exaggeration to say that there are more stabbing, slashing, pounding, rhythmically distorting accents in Beethoven's music than in the music of all his predecessors put together. According to legend, Beethoven's last act in this world was to awaken from a coma in the midst of a thunderstorm and shake his fist at the heavens. He had been doing the same in his music, on and off, for most of his life. Beethoven was the most dramatic composer who ever lived.

> Beethoven was the most dramatic composer who ever lived.

He was also the first for whom the overt expression of emotion was the most consistent guiding principle of his music. Where the resolution of related contrasts was the chief (and most Utopian) principle of the Classical sonata, in Beethoven the central issue is characteristically the resolution, or otherwise, of conflict. In his greatest tragic works, such as the turbulent "Appassionata" Sonata, the tensions are not resolved, and Utopia doesn't get a look-in. In the most serene of his late works, as in the closing movement of his last piano sonata, the tensions are not merely resolved but eliminated altogether, leaving us in a world of transcendent spiritual purity.

Beethoven's mature works fall roughly into three periods, conventionally referred to as early (c. 1790–1803), middle (c. 1803–1815), and late (c. 1815–1826). Broadly speaking, the early period is that in which he works predominantly within the heritage of the Classical tradition; the middle period embraces the so-called "heroic" decade in which he expanded and deepened the major Classical forms of the sonata, the string quartet, and the symphony to what many regarded as their formal and dramatic limits, and stretched the technical demands of his instrumental works beyond the reach of all but the most accomplished amateurs; the late period combines a transcendent spirituality, an increased preoccupation with counterpoint, and a new emphasis on formal and thematic unity within multimovement works. But these can only be used as generalizations, since within each period are a number of works that include the characteristics of other periods. In any case, neither art nor life is so neat.

Music for Solo Piano

Although Beethoven was a violinist and violist of professional caliber, the piano was his main instrument, and his works for it, especially the thirty-two piano sonatas, form the bedrock on which the bulk of the nineteenth-century repertoire was based. The great pianist and conductor Hans von Bülow famously described Bach's *Well-Tempered Clavier* as the Old Testament of music and Beethoven's sonatas as the New. Few would argue with him. With the exception of his last four years, Beethoven's piano works cover his entire life as a composer. They serve as a kind of diary of the soul, and provide a record of the most adventurous and influential journey in the history of music.

The Sonatas

It is significant that in the first three sonatas of Op. 2 (as in the three trios of **Op. 1**) Beethoven already adopts the four-movement plan of the Classical symphony. It is significant not only because it reveals from the outset that this is a man who "thinks big," but because he tended throughout his life to treat the piano as a surrogate orchestra. The wide spacings between the hands, the frequent use of massive, densely packed chords in the lower register, the unprecedented extremes of loud and soft, the use of silence as a major structural and dramatic device (ironically, his "silences" often have the impact of hammer blows): all these are characteristics that recur again and again in his piano writing.

A perfect demonstration of this powerfully rhythmic use of silence is the slow movement of the Fourth Sonata, Op. 7 in E flat, a great work second in length only to the colossal "Hammerklavier" of Beethoven's late years. Op. 10 is another trilogy, of which Nos 1 and 2, in C minor and F major, are splendidly accomplished and characterful, the former alternately stormy and lyrical, the latter a little festival of wit, good humor, and nonchalant craftsmanship. The Third Sonata of Op. 10, in D, however, is a masterpiece of symphonic scope whose four movements find Beethoven at his most commanding. The real heart of the work is the slow movement, a study in melancholy so desolate that the following minuet emerges into the light like a prisoner unexpectedly released from a dungeon, unbelieving at first, then gradually finding his feet and exulting in his newfound liberty. The work has all the drama of a great opera in a fraction of the time.

In the **"Pathétique" Sonata, Op. 13**, always among his most popular works, Beethoven once again draws on symphonic models (and Haydn's symphonies in particular) in his use of a substantial slow introduction. The powerful, dramatic opening movement is the first in which Beethoven made significant alterations to Classical sonata form. Repeatedly, at strategically placed moments, he brings back the slow introduction—or significant, fragmentary developments of it. With its beautiful, long-spun melody, the slow movement reminds us that Beethoven the wrestler with fate was also a profoundly lyrical composer, whose big, singing tone at the piano was remarked on by everyone who heard him.

The two relatively small sonatas of Op. 14 are altogether lighter fare, full of lyrical good cheer, witty conversational exchanges, and innocent romps. They are a timely reminder, after the angst of the "Pathétique," that Beethoven was also a master of light music, a born entertainer who also happened to be a genius.

> With its beautiful, long-spun melody, the slow movement reminds us that Beethoven the wrestler with fate was also a profoundly lyrical composer.

The Sonata in B flat, Op. 22, marks a return to the grand scale of Op. 2, Op. 7, and Op. 10 No. 3, but has never been a popular favorite. Written in 1800, it can be seen as Beethoven's festive farewell to the formal niceties of the eighteenth-century sonata. He seems rather to be thumbing his nose at those who were alarmed by the originality and daring of the "Pathétique." In fact, he makes such a show of being on his best behavior that the average listener can easily feel sidelined by this subtle and witty sonata.

The so-called "Funeral March" Sonata in A flat, Op. 26, an altogether different proposition, is significant on several counts. Like Mozart's well-known A major Sonata, K.331, it begins not with the usual sonata-form movement but with a gentle, gradually intensifying set of variations. This is followed by a fiery scherzo, which would normally be expected to come third; and this is succeeded in turn by a somber

Funeral March, complete with programmatic representations of drumrolls and ritual gunfire. The alternately lyrical and turbulent finale is rather in the nature of a study, which evaporates at the end into thin air. No great sonata had yet been laid out in such an unconventional manner.

The two sonatas of Op. 27 (the second being the ever-popular "Moonlight") are still less conventional. The four movements of the E flat Sonata, Op. 27 No. 1 (not one of which is in sonata form) are thematically linked and played without a break—a hitherto unheard-of procedure. This sonata may bring us very close to the character of Beethoven's renowned improvisations. In the "Moonlight," the famous first movement belongs to no previously established form, though it contains elements of sonata form. The gentle second movement is an individual take on the Classical minuet and trio; and it is only with the stormy finale that Beethoven writes a movement in full sonata form.

> In the "Moonlight," the famous first movement belongs to no previously established form, though it contains elements of sonata form.

Unlike its neighbors on either side, Sonata in D, Op. 28, is one of Beethoven's relatively neglected gems. Nicknamed the "Pastoral" (though not by Beethoven), it is among the sunniest of all the sonatas, and the scherzo is one of the most good-humored. The composer himself was especially fond of the *Andante*, but most listeners are likely to regard the rest of the movements with equal favor.

Of the three sonatas in Op. 31 (1802), the most familiar is the middle one, the so-called "Tempest" Sonata, whose opening movement, with its returning introduction, recalls the similar device used in the "Pathétique." The most revolutionary touches here, however, are the long pedal markings with their intentional "blurring" and mixing of clashing harmonies—a pretty audacious stroke at the time, which retains its sense of modernity even today.

As happens elsewhere in Beethoven's output, the two sonatas in G minor and G major, Op. 49 bear a misleading opus number. Though placed between the three sonatas of Op. 31 and the "Waldstein" of 1804, they were actually composed in 1795–7. Their appearance in the cycle is surprising not so much for stylistic reasons as for their extreme brevity (two short movements each) and the fact that they are the only ones that can be played with relative ease by near-beginners. But as with Mozart's "miniatures" and "easy" sonatas, only true artists can reveal the finesse and mastery that lie within them. The G major Sonata is interesting historically in that it marks the first appearance, in the minuet second movement, of a theme made famous by its use (in slightly amended form) in Beethoven's runaway hit of 1799, the Septet in E flat, Op. 20.

The most famous of the middle-period sonatas after the "Moonlight" are the great C major, Op. 53 (nicknamed the "Waldstein," after its dedicatee, Beethoven's patron Count Waldstein) and the F minor **"Appassionata," Op. 57**. In both of them, virtuosity reaches new heights. The "Waldstein" is perhaps the grandest and most spacious of all the sonatas so far, and was conceived and worked out at roughly the same time as Beethoven was expanding the symphony to previously unimagined proportions in the **"Eroica."** In their sound-world alone, both sonatas achieve unprecedented effects, one of the most memorable being the poetically "blurry" pedaling in the finale of the "Waldstein." Spiritually, the two works are poles apart: the "Waldstein" is one of Beethoven's most joyous and heroically invigorating works, while the "Appassionata" is a rare example of almost unmitigated tragedy. Never before had the piano been entrusted with so much tumultuous emotion. The tragedy and tumult are all the more affecting for the poignant beauty of the slow movement, whose repose is ripped apart by a single dissonant chord that leads straight into the

shocking intensity of the final, doomed struggle. Indeed, Beethoven was now writing beyond the capacities not only of most pianists but of the piano itself. In doing so, he was effectively forcing the pace of the instrument's evolution.

Composed in 1804, the same year as the "Waldstein," the short Sonata in F major, Op. 54, is one of the least played of all. Here we find Beethoven reverting to the two-movement design of the tiny sonata Op. 49. But here the resemblance ends. Challenging both technically and musically, the first movement of Op. 54, marked "In tempo d'un Menuetto," has an opening subject vaguely suggestive of Scottish folksong; the melody also has obvious links with the second subject of the "Appassionata." The second movement, by contrast, is an almost crazily obsessive study in "perpetual motion" that harks back to the finale of the A flat Sonata, Op. 26.

Where the piano is concerned, the E flat Sonata, Op. 81a (subtitled "Das Lebewohl" but usually known by the French title, "Les Adieux"), is doubly significant. At a superficial level it follows a programmatic plan, its three movements commemorating, respectively, the departure, the absence and the return of his friend and pupil the Archduke Rudolph. The word "Lebewohl" ("farewell") is spelled out over the three-note descending "motto" of the opening, which is periodically recalled in the following *Allegro*. Apart from being one of the richest and most instantly attractive works in the cycle, it marked Beethoven's farewell to the piano sonata for a period of five years, and indeed a farewell to his "heroic" middle period. The next sonata–No. 27 in E minor, Op. 90, in two movements– dates from 1814 and stands on the threshold of his third period.

In the view of many musicians, the last five piano sonatas (Opp. 101, 106, and 109–**111**) are the greatest ever written. Op. 101 in A major is a notably concentrated four-movement work, to a slow–fast–slow–fast pattern, in which the lyrical, ruminative

opening of the first movement returns to introduce the grandly assertive fugal finale (which has echoes of Beethoven's beloved Handel). Like all the late sonatas, the work is highly serious; but this does not preclude a number of typically self-mocking jokes in the midst of the generally imposing finale. And the obsessive dotted rhythms of the second-movement March (te-tum te-tum te-tum, etc.) seem directly to anticipate Schumann.

Op. 106 in B flat, the so-called "Hammerklavier," is the longest, most taxing and most awesomely imposing sonata ever written. The sonata's nickname is merely the German name for the piano, and the inscription "für das Hammerklavier" appears on the title pages of both Op. 101 and Op. 109. But there is no doubt that it is in this B flat sonata that the klavier gets the greatest hammering. How the pianos of Beethoven's day could withstand it is hard to imagine. Not that many had to: Beethoven was already writing for later generations and did not expect the public of his own time to understand it. For many musicians it only confirmed their belief that Beethoven, isolated by deafness, had gone mad. The fantastically difficult and extended fugue that crowns the work is in many ways as daunting, as rawly elemental and as stupendously sophisticated today as it ever was.

> For many musicians it only confirmed their belief that Beethoven, isolated by deafness, had gone mad.

The last three sonatas, Opp. 109, 110, and **111**, take us onto hallowed ground. Each creates a universe all its own, each defies meaningful description. Each takes us on a spiritual odyssey into uncharted regions of the soul, into realms of experience we could never previously have imagined.

The Variations

Beethoven wrote variations at every stage of his life, many in separate, self-contained sets, some incorporated into sonatas.

They range from the merely attractive (some of the juvenilia) to the towering "Diabelli" Variations, Op. 120—his last great piano work—and the variations in the sonatas Opp. 109 and 111). Curiously, one of Beethoven's most frequently played sets of variations is among his least interesting: the 32 Variations on an Original Theme in C minor. In all but the most exceptional hands, these too easily sound like a sequence of high-class exercises *à la* Hanon or Czerny. More engaging and less obvious are the clever and sometimes amusing sets on *Rule, Britannia* and *God Save the King*, but there are only three sets that give us really vintage Beethoven. The first of these is the interestingly titled Six Variations in F major, Op. 34—interesting because only the last of the variations is in that key (indeed, no two variations share the same key). Next comes a really great set, written at the same time (1802) and usually known today as the "Eroica" Variations because the theme is the same as that of the finale of the "Eroica" Symphony. In fact the piano work predates the symphony. There is nothing forbidding here, but plenty in the way of grandeur, invention, virtuosity, and humor. Indeed, even the theme is humorous, with its coy sounding of the principal notes and the rude interruptions where Beethoven seems to mock his own seriousness. It is one of the most appealing aspects of Beethoven's character that his sense of humor continually crops up in the most unexpected contexts. A striking case in point is his last major piano work, the "Diabelli" Variations, whose monumentality does not preclude an abundance of typical Beethoven jokes. The way he mocks the trivial theme in the first variation is bullying raised to the level of high art. A more merciless kick in the teeth was never delivered by a great composer to a small one. Having thus sorted out the men from the boys, Beethoven proceeds to build from this "cobbler's patch" (his own description of Diabelli's little waltz) a gigantic edifice of overwhelming intellectual power and emotional range. According to the composer himself, the work is also a compendium of everything he knew about piano technique.

Chapter 2

Crisis

Crisis

As the eighteenth century drew to a close, Beethoven, then in his mid-twenties and riding on the crest of a wave, had made a terrifying discovery. For the better part of two years he kept it to himself, though it brought about changes in his behavior that must have baffled his friends. The first time he divulged his secret was in a letter to a friend in Bonn, Franz Wegeler—a doctor, as it happened:

Beethoven, aged 28, by Josef Kreihuber, 1865

That jealous demon, my health, has thrown a mean spoke in my wheel: for some time my hearing *has been growing progressively weaker—on top of which my ears now hum and buzz continuously day and night. And my abdomen, which was ever in a wretched state, has also grown steadily worse. The truth is that in spite of my great successes I have been leading a most miserable existence. For two years I have avoided almost all social gatherings because it is impossible for me to say to people, "I am deaf." If I belonged to any other profession it would be easier, but in my profession it is a truly dreadful state.*

Dreadful enough to have driven a number of similarly afflicted musicians insane: Smetana, in a later generation of composers, was a particularly famous case.

However much Beethoven may have tried to conceal his deafness, it was only a matter of time before it would be obvious to everyone. Ferdinand Ries, a pupil and close friend who was destined to be a successful composer, recalled with a terrible poignancy the day *he* first noticed it:

> *Beethoven took particular pleasure in wandering through the countryside. One day we set out happily together and soon found ourselves in lonely woods on the beautiful mountain slopes of Baden. After having walked for about an hour, we sat down to rest in the grass. Suddenly, from the slope on the other side of the valley, came the sound of a shepherd's pipe, whose unexpected melody under the clear blue sky, in the deep solitude of the woods, made a remarkable impression on me. Since Beethoven was sitting next to me, I commented on this. The sounds continued so bright and clear that it was not possible to miss a single note. He listened, but I was able to see from his expression that he had heard nothing. In order not to sadden or alarm him, I pretended that I too could no longer hear them. But the sweet fascination which these sounds had exercised on me at first now turned into a feeling of the most profound sadness. Almost without realizing it, I walked along silently, sunk in sad thoughts, at the side of my great master, who, as before, was occupied with his own inner meditations, continuing to hum indistinguishable phrases and tones, and to sing aloud. When after several hours we returned home, he sat down impatiently at the piano and exclaimed, almost angrily, "Now I shall play something for you." With irresistible fire and mighty force he played what was later to become the Allegro of the great Sonata* **"Appassionata."** *That is a day which will remain forever etched upon my mind.*

CD 1
track 6

www.naxos.com

Almost as though it had been planned from on high, the dawn of the nineteenth century saw a major upswing in Beethoven's

Prince Karl Lichnowsky, benefactor

fortunes as a composer. By comparison, the successes of the previous decade began to seem like little more than a glorious introduction. In 1800 he was relieved of financial anxieties by an annuity from Prince Lichnowsky, in whose home he was then living. In the spring of that year he gave an immensely successful concert of his own works, one of which, the splendid Septet in E flat, Op. 20, became, as Beethoven saw it, so disproportionately popular that he began to regret having written it.

Despite the sale of his works and the generous annuity from Lichnowsky, Beethoven devoted a certain amount of his time to teaching. It was at around this time that the ten-year-old Carl Czerny was taken to audition for him:

> *After gaining admission to the house in which Beethoven was living, my father and I climbed up, as if in a tower, to the sixth floor, where a rather grubby-looking servant announced us to Beethoven and then showed us in. We found ourselves in a very barren-looking room, papers and clothes strewn all over the place, a few boxes, bare walls, hardly a single chair, save for a rickety one by the piano. Beethoven was dressed in a jacket of some shaggy dark grey cloth, and trousers of the same material, so that he immediately reminded me of Robinson Crusoe, which I had just then read. The coal-black hair, cut rather in the style of a Roman emperor, stood up around his head. His black beard, unshaven for several days, darkened the lower part of his already dark-complexioned face. Also, I noticed at a glance, as*

children are wont to do, that his ears were stuffed with cotton wool which seemed to have been dipped in some yellow fluid. Yet at the time not the slightest sign of deafness was apparent. His hands were very hairy, and his fingers, especially at the tips, were unusually broad... I played to him his own **"Pathétique" Sonata***, after which he turned to my father and said, "The boy has talent. I will teach him."*

The "Pathétique" Sonata was in some ways the most revolutionary work Beethoven had yet produced—sufficiently so, indeed, to alarm the more conservative of Vienna's many piano teachers, who warned their pupils against it. For many of their more advanced pupils, on the other hand, this was the most exciting keyboard work ever written. Among these was Ignaz Moscheles, later an excellent composer and one of the foremost pianists of his day:

At this time I heard from some of my fellow pupils that there was a young composer in Vienna who wrote the most extraordinary stuff, which no one could either play or understand—a highly developed music in conflict with all the rules. This composer's name, I learned, was Beethoven. When I went to the circulating library in order to satisfy my curiosity about this eccentric genius, I found his "Pathétique" Sonata. Since my pocket money did not suffice to buy it, I secretly copied it out. The novelty of the style fascinated me, and I was seized by such an enthusiastic admiration of it that I went so far as to forget myself and tell my teacher about my new discovery. This gentleman reminded me of his instructions and warned me against playing or studying such wild and eccentric productions. I paid no attention, and found in Beethoven's music such consolation, pleasure, and excitement as no other composer had ever given me.

There is an interesting discrepancy at this point in his life between Beethoven's revolutionary compositions and his approach to teaching, which was surprisingly conservative. His condition for teaching Czerny was that the boy be equipped with C.P.E. Bach's treatise *On the True Art of Keyboard Playing*, published almost twenty years before Beethoven was born. Beethoven had little time for most of the treatises written subsequently, and intended for many years to write one of his own. Pianists can only lament that he never got around to it. Its absence makes the recollections of his pupils all the more tantalizing. We return to Czerny:

> *During the first lessons, Beethoven kept me altogether on scales in all the keys, and showed me (something at the time still unknown to most players) the only correct position of the hands and fingers and, in particular, how to use the thumb, rules whose usefulness I did not learn fully to appreciate until a much later date. Then he went over the studies belonging to this method with me and, especially, called my attention to the* legato, *which he himself controlled to such an incomparable degree, and which at that time all other pianists regarded as impossible of execution on the fortepiano, for even after Mozart's day, the choppy, short, detached manner of playing was the fashion. In later years, Beethoven himself told me that he had heard Mozart play on various occasions and that Mozart, since at the time the invention of the fortepiano was still in its infancy, had accustomed himself to a mode of playing on the claviers then more frequently used, which was in no way adapted to the fortepiano. In the course of time I also made the acquaintance of several persons who had taken lessons from Mozart, and found this remark justified by their playing.*

This is baffling, as it flies in the face of Mozart's own words, written out rather than passed down by hearsay, to the effect that piano-playing should "flow like oil."

Czerny continues: "He also was satisfied with my sight-reading, after he had given me the manuscript of his Sonata in C major, Op. 35 [sic] to play. From that time forward Beethoven was favorably inclined toward me and treated me in a friendly manner to the end of his days." Beethoven's own sight-reading, however, as Czerny reports, was of another order altogether:

> *It was astonishing how he could take in compositions at a glance—even manuscripts and large scores—and how well he played them! In this respect he had no equal. His manner of interpreting them was always decisive, but sharp and hard. The same praise is due his presentation of the great masters' compositions: he played Handel's oratorios and Gluck's works wonderfully well, thereby earning the greatest applause. This also holds good of Sebastian Bach's fugues.*

Another pupil of Beethoven's at around this time, Countess Giulietta Guicciardi, left a contrasting impression of his approach, disconcertingly written in the third person, then a fashionable affectation:

> *He allowed her to play his compositions, but he was exceedingly severe with her until her interpretation was correct to the very last tiny detail. He insisted on a light touch, but he himself was often violent, throwing the music around and tearing it up. He would accept no payment, though he was very poor, but accepted linen under the pretext that it had been hand-sewn by the Countess. In the same way, he taught Princess Odescalchi and Baroness Ertmann; they came to him or he went to them. He did not like to play his own compositions, but cared only to improvise. At the least sound [from his listeners] he would abruptly arise and depart.*

A third pupil from the period was Ferdinand Ries, a fellow émigré from Bonn. In his valuable reminiscences, written many years later, he confirms that Beethoven taught no two people in quite the same way. While no pupil could escape Beethoven's anger entirely, Ries was never treated to the kind of temper tantrums lavished on the Countess:

When Beethoven gave me a lesson he was, I might almost say, unnaturally patient. Thus he often would have me repeat a single number ten or more times. In the Variations in F major, Op. 34, I was obliged to repeat almost the entire final Adagio *variation seventeen times; and even then he was not satisfied with the expression in the small cadenza, though I thought I played it as well as he did [!]. That day I had almost a two-hour lesson. When I left out something in a passage, a note or a skip, which in many cases he wished to have specially emphasized, or if I struck a wrong key, he seldom said anything; yet when I was at fault with regard to the* expression, *the crescendi, or matters of that kind, or in the character of the piece, he would grow angry. Mistakes of the other kind, he said, were due to chance; but these last resulted from want of knowledge, feeling, or attention. He himself often made mistakes of the first kind, even when playing in public.*

Beethoven's public performances at that time were revelatory, giving as yet no hint of the havoc being played with his hearing. As Anton Schindler recalled, citing a specific instance:

What the **Sonata "Pathétique"** *was in Beethoven's hands was something one had to hear repeatedly in order to be quite certain that it was the same already well-known work. Every single thing became, in his hands, a new creation, in which his always* legato *playing, one of the particular characteristics of his execution, played an important part.*

There was no hint in his output of the crisis that was to engulf him. His hearing apart, 1800 was a good year for Beethoven. During it he completed the **First Symphony** and the six quartets, Op. 18, composed the Piano Sonata in B flat, Op. 22, and the Sonata for horn and piano (an instant hit), and began the Third Piano Concerto and the ballet music *The Creatures of Prometheus*.

If the harvest of Beethoven's works in 1800 had been impressive, it was all but dwarfed by his achievements in 1801. He scored his greatest success yet with *The Creatures of Prometheus*, he composed two of his finest violin sonatas, Opp. 23 and 24 (the famous "Spring" Sonata), the String Quintet in C, Op. 29, and four of his groundbreaking piano sonatas, including Op. 26, with its Funeral March, Op. 28 "Pastoral" (for some time his own favorite of his piano works to date), and the so-called "Moonlight" Sonata[1]. This was not entirely unrelated to the fact that he was in love. As he wrote to a friend that autumn:

> *I am now living a more agreeable life, inasmuch as I go about more among my fellow men. You cannot imagine how empty, how sad my life has been for the last two years. My weak hearing haunted me every-where, like a ghost, and so I avoided people. The change has been brought about by a lovable charming girl who loves me and whom I love. So after two years I enjoy a few happy moments, and this is the first time I feel that marriage could bring happiness with it. Unfortu-nately, I am not of her class, and now—I naturally could not marry—I must somehow keep going as best I can.*

The "lovable, charming girl" was none other than the beautiful seventeen-year-old Countess Giulietta Guicciardi, whom we have already encountered as his pupil.

Beethoven was often in love, but almost invariably with women who were unavailable, whether for reasons of class, or age, or the more usual fact that they were already married. We have no evidence that Giulietta was also in love with Beethoven; but more than twenty years later he returned to the subject, more insistent than ever. "It is perfectly true," he wrote. "I was very much loved by her—far more than her husband ever was." Perhaps—though her description of him as being "very

---

[1] Not so called by Beethoven. The nickname comes from the poet and critic Ludwig Rellstab's remark that the first movement reminded him of "moonlight reflected on the waters of Lake Lucerne."

ugly, and most of the time very shabbily dressed" is less than a ringing endorsement of the claim. In any case, it was to her that he dedicated the "Moonlight." This remains probably the most famous sonata ever written, partly due to the fact that its evocative first movement is relatively easy to play.

His prolific output of one masterpiece after another suggests that Beethoven's return to society, spurred by his love for Giulietta, and what he took to be her love for him, acted on him like a bracing tonic. As a composer he was on a winning streak, and he exulted in it:

> *Ah! I feel that my youth is just beginning! My physical strength has for some time past been steadily gaining, and with it my mental powers. Each day I move a little further towards the goal which I sense but cannot describe. Grant me but half freedom from my affliction, and you will see me as happy as it is possible to be!*

In 1802, the winning streak continued. From it came the three Op. 30 sonatas for violin and piano, the three piano sonatas, Op. 31 (including the "Tempest"), the "Eroica" Variations, Op. 35, the Six Variations in F, Op. 34, the first set of Bagatelles for the piano, and the high-spirited **Symphony No. 2 in D**–plainly the work of an exuberant genius brimming over with the sheer joy of being alive. If we look at the testimony of his friends, however, and at his own *verbal* writings of the same year, we get an altogether different impression.

Among the papers found in Beethoven's house after his death is a strange document written to his brothers Carl and Johann in October 1802. It has been known ever since as the "Heiligenstadt Testament," Heiligenstadt being the suburb of Vienna where Beethoven was staying at the time. An immensely long letter, amounting in effect to a will, it is in many ways the most revealing and disturbing verbal document he ever wrote. That being so, it is printed here in its entirety. Its strangeness is already evident in its heading, where Beethoven leaves an empty space in place of Johann's name. This cannot be an oversight, for he does the same thing twice more:

FOR MY BROTHERS CARL AND   *BEETHOVEN*

Oh ye men who think or say that I am malevolent, stubborn, or mis-anthropic, how greatly do you wrong me. You do not know the secret cause which makes me seem that way to you. From childhood on, my heart and soul have been full of the tender feeling of goodwill, and I was ever inclined to accomplish great things. But think that for six

Beethoven's house in Heiligenstadt

years now I have been hopelessly afflicted, made worse by senseless physicians, from year to year deceived with hopes of improvement, finally compelled to face the prospect of a lasting malady (whose cure will take years or, perhaps, be impossible). Though born with a fiery active temperament, even susceptible to the diversions of society, I was soon compelled to withdraw myself, to live life alone. If at times I tried to forget all this, oh how harshly was I flung back by the doubly sad experience of my bad hearing. Yet it was impossible for me to say to people, "Speak louder, shout, for I am deaf." Ah, how could I possibly admit an infirmity in the one sense which ought to be more perfect in me than in others, a sense which I once possessed in the highest perfection, a perfection such as few in my profession enjoy or ever have enjoyed. Oh I cannot do it; therefore forgive me when you see me draw back when I would have gladly mingled with you. My misfortune is doubly painful to me because I am bound to be misunderstood; for me there can be no relaxation with my fellow men, no refined conversations, no mutual exchange of ideas. I must live almost alone, like one who has been banished; I can mix with society only as much as true necessity demands. If I approach near to people a hot terror seizes upon me, and I fear being exposed to the danger that my condition might be noticed. Thus it has been during the last six months which I have spent in the country. By ordering me to spare my hearing as much as possible, my intelligent doctor almost fell in with my own present frame of mind, though sometimes I ran counter to it by yielding to my desire for companionship. But what a humiliation for me when someone standing next to me heard a flute in the distance and I heard nothing, or someone heard a shepherd singing and again I heard nothing. Such incidents drove me almost to despair; a little more of that and I would have ended my life—it was only my art that held me back. Ah, it seemed to me impossible to leave the world until I had brought forth all that I felt was within me. So I endured this wretched existence—truly wretched for so susceptible a body, which can be thrown by a sudden change from the best condition to the very

> "Oh how harshly was I flung back by the doubly sad experience of my bad hearing."

worst. Patience, *they say, is what I must now choose for my guide, and I have done so. I hope my determination will remain firm to endure until it pleases the inexorable Parcae to break the thread. Perhaps I shall get better, perhaps not; I am ready. Forced to become a philosopher already in my twenty-eighth year—oh it is not easy, and for the artist much more difficult than for anyone else.*

Divine One, Thou seest my inmost soul; Thou knowest that therein dwells the love of mankind and the desire to do good. Oh fellow men, when at some point you read this, consider then that you have done me an injustice; someone who has had misfortune may console himself to find a similar case to his, who despite all the limitations of Nature nevertheless did everything within his powers to become accepted among worthy artists and men. You, my brothers Carl and   , as soon as I am dead, if Dr Schmidt is still alive, ask him in my name to describe my malady, and attach this written document to his account of my illness so that so far as is possible at least the world may become reconciled to me after my death. At the same time, I declare you two to be the heirs to my small fortune (if so it can be called); divide it fairly; bear with and help each other. What injury you have done me you know was long ago forgiven. To you, brother Carl, I give special thanks for the attachment you have shown me of late. It is my wish that you may have a better and freer life than I have had. Recommend virtue to your children; it alone, not money, can make them happy. I speak from experience; this was what upheld me in time of misery. Thanks to it and to my art, I did not end my life by suicide.

Farewell and love each other—I thank all my friends, particularly Prince Lichnowsky and Professor Schmidt—I would like the instruments from Prince L. to be preserved by one of you, but not to be the cause of strife between you, and as soon as they can serve you a better purpose, then sell them. How happy I shall be if I can still be helpful to you in my grave—so be it. With joy I hasten to meet death— if it comes before I have had the chance to develop all my artistic capacities, it will still be coming too soon despite my harsh fate, and I should probably wish it later—yet even so I should be happy, for would it not free me, from a state of endless suffering?—Come when Thou wilt! I shall meet Thee bravely. Farewell and do not wholly forget me when I am dead; I deserve this from you, for during my lifetime I was thinking of you often and of ways to make you happy—be ye so.

LUDWIG VAN BEETHOVEN (seal)

Heiglnstadt [sic] October 6, 1802

Four days later, he adds a postscript:

Heiligenstadt, October 10, 1802, thus I bid thee farewell—and indeed sadly. Yes, that fond hope—which I brought here with me, to be cured to a degree at least—this I must now wholly abandon. As the leaves of autumn fall and are withered—so likewise has my hope been blighted— I leave here—almost as I came—even the high courage—which often inspired me in the beautiful days of summer—has disappeared. Oh Providence—grant me at last but one day of pure joy—it is so long since real joy echoed in my heart—Oh when—Oh when, Oh Divine One— shall I feel it again in the temple of nature and of mankind—Never?— No—Oh that would be too hard.

For my brothers Carl and   , to be read and executed after my death.

The immediate cause of these despairing words was obviously the loss of his hearing. And though no one could reasonably doubt the reality of his suffering, it should be mentioned, if only for historical accuracy, that until his final few years Beethoven's deafness was not as absolute as posterity has chosen to believe. Nevertheless, it *was* a cruel and deeply unsettling affliction, and there is evidence, not only in the

"Heiligenstadt Testament" but in the testimony of his friends, that it may well have driven him to the brink of suicide. Some claim that he actually attempted it, but the evidence is slim.

Whatever one makes of the "Heiligenstadt Testament," Beethoven was experiencing a crisis of gigantic proportions.

Interlude II:
Chamber Music (1): Mixed Families

Piano Plus

Although the early quartets for piano and string trio are engaging, Beethoven's first major chamber works were the three piano trios, **Op. 1** (piano, violin, and cello). Even here, at the formal beginning of his career as a composer, he was a master wholly fit to stand beside his teacher Haydn. Quite apart from their mastery, however, they are notable for their liberation of the cello, which in Haydn's trios seldom did more than double the left hand of the piano part. Also significant is Beethoven's adoption of the spacious four-movement plan normally associated with the Classical symphony—a plan chosen for all but one of his subsequent trios. The last of the Op. 1 trios, in C minor, is notable for being the most intensely emotional and dramatic piano trio written to date (Haydn reportedly found it downright alarming).

> Its atmosphere and textures are unique, its originality is breathtaking, and its dark emotions haunt the mind long after the music has ceased.

Among the later trios, two require special mention. Op. 70 No. 1 in D major is a magnificent work whose astounding, eerie slow movement may well be the slowest slow movement ever written. Its atmosphere and textures are unique, its originality is breathtaking, and its dark emotions haunt the mind long after the music has ceased. Not for nothing is this trio widely known as the "Ghost." It does not always follow that last works are best, but in the case of Beethoven's final piano trio, the so-called **"Archduke," Op. 97**, there can be no argument. For sustained inspiration, formal mastery, and spiritual depth, it remains unsurpassed.

The first of Beethoven's instrumental duos, the two wonderful cello sonatas, Op. 5, are historically important as well as artistically captivating. In addition to their intrinsic worth, they are the first works of their kind. Haydn and Mozart wrote superb cello parts in their string quartets but left no sonatas for the instrument. The only (distant) precedents among great composers were the three sonatas by Bach for viola da gamba and harpsichord. Of Beethoven's remaining cello sonatas, the A major, Op. 69, has always been the most popular with cellists and audiences alike, above all for its spacious, serenely lyrical first movement. Most musicians, however, would agree that the greatest are the two late sonatas, Op. 102. These are more austere and cerebral than Op. 69, with an emphasis on close contrapuntal textures; both demand exceptional concentration from the listener, particularly the second, in D, which inhabits something of the same craggy world as the "Hammerklavier" Sonata for piano.

The largest group of Beethoven's duo works is formed by the ten violin sonatas. While the piano was Beethoven's main instrument, he was also a very competent violinist, and it shows. Each sonata finds him exploring the potentialities of the violin in different ways, and each is a developing study in the relationship between the violin and the piano. Even when he gives the violin apparently simple accompanying figures, they are never merely accompanimental, but enrich the musical blend. Beethoven sometimes uses the violin (as in the slow movement of the E flat Sonata, Op. 12 No. 3) as a kind of alternative to the pianist's left hand, demanding the most sensitive listening on the part of both players. At other times (say, the third variation in the D major Sonata, Op. 12 No. 1), he may stretch the character of the violin by asking it to rival the turbulence and percussive rhythmic profile of the piano. Beethoven's sometimes explosive emotional realism led to his becoming the first great composer who repeatedly enlisted an element of struggle, even harshness, as an agent of expression. There are moments in Beethoven where to play beautifully can be downright unmusical. The violin sonatas show the same sort of progress away from the expected and traditional as one finds in the symphonies, the quartets and the piano sonatas. It can fairly be said that Beethoven made the violin a "bigger" instrument than anyone had previously imagined, most famously in the "Kreutzer" Sonata, Op. 47. Here, drama, virtuosity, and intellect are inextricably combined and raised to a level never before achieved in the medium. As in practically every other medium he touched, he brought to the violin sonata an unprecedented emotional and dramatic range.

> Those who deplore the phenomenon of muzak should be partially consoled to learn that the concept was not born yesterday.

Music for Wind

Most of Beethoven's chamber music involving wind instruments dates from his Bonn years and his early years in Vienna. Those who deplore the phenomenon of muzak—purpose-built background music in restaurants, elevators, shopping malls, and so on—should be partially consoled to learn that the concept was not born yesterday. Background music is as old as music itself. At the height of the Baroque era, composers commonly wrote music specifically designed to be talked to, served to, poured to—anything but listened to, and often out of doors.

Much of the music of Georg Philipp Telemann was entitled *Tafelmusik* ("Table Music"). Music for similar purposes was written by Haydn and Mozart, who regularly exceeded their brief. Beethoven did likewise as court musician to the Elector Max Franz at Bonn, whose "household" included a small wind band of two oboes, two clarinets, two horns, and two bassoons. It was for just such an ensemble, in 1792, that Beethoven wrote his Octet in E flat major, misleadingly tagged Op. 103, and the Rondino in E flat major, WoO25 ("WoO" indicates a work without opus no.). For music composed to be played out of doors, wind instruments, with their penetrating tone and variety of color, were preferable to the mellower and more homogeneous strings. The Octet in particular, in striking contrast to Beethoven's later recasting of it as a string quintet, is tailormade to cope both with the elements and the noisiest of banquets. Boisterous *tutti*s (full ensemble) and frequent markings of *fortissimo* combine with gentler movements to provide musical entertainment of a high order. Beethoven keeps his players happy, too, by showcasing their skills, as with the oboe in the slow movement, the clarinet in the finale, and the fanfare of horns at the end. Other enjoyable works of this period include the Sextet in E flat, Op. 71 for two each of clarinets, oboes, horns, and bassoons, and the even better Sextet in E flat, Op. 81b (another misleadingly high opus number) for two horns and string quartet.

As may be becoming apparent, Beethoven in his twenties seems to have been abnormally partial to the key of E flat, especially where chamber music is concerned. In addition to the works already discussed, we have in that key three piano trios (one of them a single movement), one string trio, an *Adagio* for piano and mandolin (!), one violin sonata, a duet for viola and cello, the Quintet for Piano and Wind, Op. 16, the great Piano Sonata, Op. 7 and the Septet, Op. 20. Of these, the last three stand out from all the rest (for comment on Op. 7, see p. 24). The Quintet for Piano and Wind would seem to have been directly modeled on Mozart's K.452, also in E flat, which he regarded as the best of all his works to date.

The elimination of a second violin in favor of a double bass was a stroke of genius.

Beethoven's, by general consent, is not in that class; but it is a fine composition nevertheless, and one of his most popular chamber works. Interestingly, soon after finishing it, Beethoven arranged it as a quartet for piano and strings. This is hardly ever played, which is a pity. It has been felt by some that the strings, with their homogeneity of tone, are less suited than the original winds to the lengthy, conversational introduction, and that the absence of the horn, in particular, from the "hunting" finale is a near-fatal drawback.

If any one work were to be selected as Beethoven's number one hit in the realm of chamber music, it would have to be the Septet in E flat for violin, viola, cello, double bass, clarinet, horn, and bassoon. Composed in 1799 and a roaring success ever since, it lays no claim to being a profound work. It is, though, one of the most sheerly delightful chamber works ever written; and it gives early notice of Beethoven's genius for combining contrasting tone colors in a manner that seems not only natural but inevitable. One gets some measure of its impact at the time from the fact that Schubert was commissioned by a wealthy amateur clarinettist, Count Ferdinand Troyer, to write a work as similar as possible to Beethoven's Septet. The result was a great work, the Octet in F, which, while similar in instrumentation (save for the addition of a second violin), is Schubert through and through. As with Rachmaninov's Prelude in C sharp minor, the Septet became so popular that its composer sometimes rued the day he ever wrote it. It remains, nevertheless, the high point of his chamber works involving wind instruments. The elimination of a second violin in favor of a double bass was a stroke of genius, providing a firm basis in sound for the blending of winds, brass, and strings above. Aware of the work's potential for amateur performance, Beethoven here avoids the kind of virtuoso instrumental solos that we find in many of his earlier chamber works. Significant, too, is his adoption of a loose, divertimento-like sequence of six movements.

With the composition of the Septet, Beethoven's apparent obsession with the key of E flat comes to an end, as does his use of wind ensembles in chamber works. This is no coincidence. The choice of E flat for all but a handful of his works for wind was strategic. For reasons of intonation too complex to go into here, E flat major was far and away the best key for drawing together his various mixtures of wind instruments, both within the family and when mixed with strings or piano.

From 1800 onward Beethoven's use of wind in his chamber works was, with one exception (an *Adagio* for three horns in 1815), confined to a single instrument. Two of these works particularly deserve mentioning. One is the Sonata for horn and piano, Op. 17; the other is the delightful Serenade in D major, Op. 25 for the unusual combination of flute, violin, and viola. Basically a six-movement divertimento, this piece is alternately concise and expansive, and finds Beethoven at his most resourceful, texturally, structurally, and instrumentally. Given the loving and idiomatic writing for the flute, it seems surprising that he used the instrument so sparingly in his music as a whole. Occasionally here, he gives the flute a rest and writes for the strings alone, sometimes allowing the viola to soar high above the violin, or using double-stops to create the fleeting impression of a string quartet. As noted earlier, Beethoven at this stage in his life was more than happy to indulge his players: witness here the virtuoso opportunities for each in the splendid finale. The two sets of National Airs with Variations for piano with optional flute or violin from 1818–19 are hardly for wind, and are little more than curiosities. Others are two works from around 1795 for two oboes and cor anglais (the latter being an instrument that he never used again, despite his obvious affection for the oboe in his orchestral music), a quintet (yet another in E flat) for oboe, three horns, and bassoon, and, most bizarre of all, four works for piano and mandolin. The most haunting and substantial of Beethoven's instrumental oddities are the three *Equali* for four trombones, composed in 1812. Two of them were memorably performed at his funeral, in an arrangement for voices.

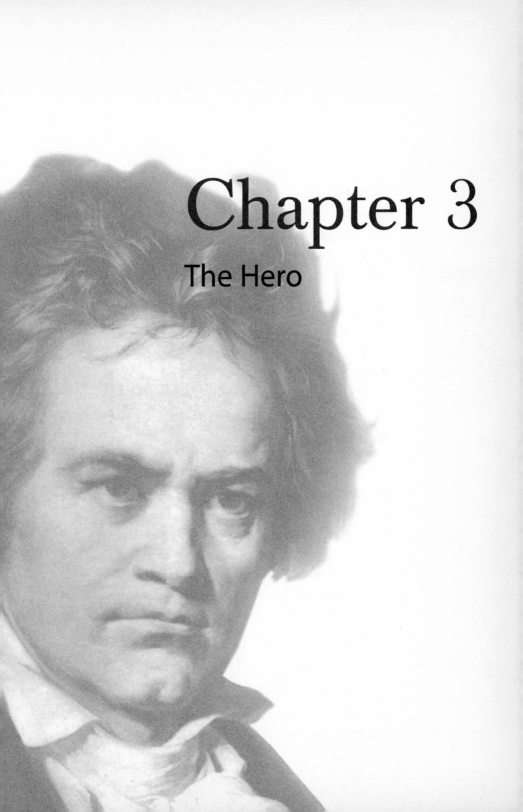

Chapter 3

The Hero

The Hero

If the "Heiligenstadt Testament" and the Second Symphony tell conflicting stories about Beethoven's innermost feelings, what can we safely deduce from his **Third Symphony, the "Eroica"**? It was originally written as a tribute to Napoleon, whom Beethoven admired at the time almost to the point of idolatry, and it was to bear his name in its title. When Napoleon proclaimed himself Emperor on May 20, 1804, Beethoven, like many of his distinguished contemporaries, felt both outraged and betrayed. Ferdinand Ries witnessed the immediate consequence:

> *I was the first person to inform him of Bonaparte's proclamation. Beethoven at once flew into a terrible rage, crying out, "So he too is nothing but an ordinary mortal. Now he will trample underfoot all the Rights of Man and indulge only his ambition. He will now set himself on high, like all the others, and become a tyrant!" With these words he crossed to his desk, seized the title page from the top, tore it up completely, and threw it on the floor. The first page was written out again, and it was only then that the work received the title* Sinfonia Eroica.

It is assumed that what Ries saw was the original manuscript, which subsequently disappeared. Given Beethoven's peculiar attitude to the autograph scores of even his greatest works, this is hardly surprising. As Ries observed at around the same time:

Beethoven attached no importance to his manuscript scores. In most cases, once they had been engraved, they lay about in an adjoining room or in the middle of his workroom, scattered over the floor among other music. I often have put his music in order, yet when Beethoven was looking for something, everything was then turned upside down again. I could at that time have carried off all those original auto-graph compositions of his which had already been engraved, and had I asked him for them, I am sure he would have given them to me with-out a moment's hesitation.

But Beethoven had not finished venting his rage against Napoleon. On the copy-ist's score, which can still be seen at the Gesellschaft der Musikfreunde in Vienna, Napoleon's name has been so forcefully erased that there is a hole in the paper. Ries's chronology, how-ever, is mistaken. When Beethoven offered the symphony to Breitkopf & Härtel a mere three months later, he specifically stated that the work's title was "Bonaparte." Only when it appeared in print did it bear the name "Eroica."

The "Eroica" can thus be seen as Beethoven's own answer to the "Heiligenstadt Testament."

In the light of what we know about Beethoven's life at the time, it seems clear that the real hero of the symphony, con-sciously or otherwise, was never really Napoleon but Beethoven himself—or, at any rate, that the work's central pre-occupation is not with any individual hero but with the nature of heroism itself, as perceived by Beethoven in the light of his own experience. The "Eroica" can thus be seen as Beethoven's own answer to the "Heiligenstadt Testament." And if its four huge movements follow any specific program, as nineteenth-century critics seem to have insisted that they must, it has to do with the heroism of confronting and transcending despair.

The "Eroica" was a major landmark not only in Beethoven's life but in the history of music. Never before had music been so obviously and overwhelmingly rooted in the individual

experience of its composer; never had it assumed such epic proportions (the first movement alone is as long as many complete
symphonies in the eighteenth century). Nor had unflinching
intellect and passionate emotion ever been married with such
inescapable logic. The sketchbooks in which Beethoven slowly,
painfully, groped his way to the ultimate truth and power of the
"Eroica" form themselves a kind of heroic document. Despite
the immensity of his genius, Beethoven was not a composer like
Mozart or Schubert, from whom inspired ideas seemed to flow
with perfect ease. From the very beginning, he was wrestler, a
man who knew that in order to succeed you need the courage to
fail. Some of his early sketches are in fact breathtakingly ordi-
nary. But slowly, laboriously, he bends these unpromising materials to his purpose. For Beethoven, struggle and composition
were almost synonymous. What makes the "Eroica" heroic is its
demonstration of the indomitable triumph of the human will.

A composer changing the course of musical history is
bound to encounter opposition, and it was with the "Eroica"
that Beethoven's hitherto loyal and enthusiastic audience
began to waver. The critic for the *Allgemeine musikalische Zeitung*
spoke for many when he wrote:

> *This long and extremely taxing work is actually a protracted, daring,*
> *and wild fantasy. There is no lack of striking and beautiful passages,*
> *which reveal the energy and talent of their creator, but more often the*
> *work appears to lose itself in anarchy. This reviewer undoubtedly*
> *belongs to Beethoven's most sincere admirers, but he must admit to*
> *finding too much here that is bizarre and shrill. An overall view is all*
> *but impossible to form, and a sense of unity is almost entirely missing.*

The sheer length and concentration of the work baffled many an
otherwise sympathetic listener, and a similarly large-scale
architectural plan began to be a feature of Beethoven's work

generally. It was not just the fickle Viennese audience who had trouble following Beethoven through his latest, uncompromising phase. Such close musical colleagues as the violinist Schuppanzigh, for instance, were baffled by the three great string quartets that Beethoven wrote for the Russian Count Razumovsky in 1806. Again, the span of the works was unprecedented (the first is almost twice the average length of a quartet by Haydn), as was the sustained emotional intensity. At thirty-five, Beethoven was already writing, as he once put it, "for a later age." He was writing pure music, straight from the heart and refined with a

Count Andreas Razumovksy (1752–1836)

ruthless concentration and intellectual control. To an extent which no previous composer had dared dream of, he was writing not for but beyond the players of his own time. When Schuppanzigh complained that a passage in one of the quartets was unplayable, Beethoven was unmoved: "What do I care for your miserable fiddle when the spirit moves me?"

Like athletes and scientists through the ages, Beethoven was pushing the frontiers of the possible beyond their known limits. He was consciously forcing the pace of musical evolution. Today, of course, musicians can play everything he wrote, without a hint of brinkmanship. The technical challenges of Beethoven's great quartets, however, are as nothing compared with the emotional and spiritual experience that they were designed to convey. In the slow movement of the **Second "Razumovsky" Quartet**, itself nearly a quarter of an hour in

CD 1
track 9

www.naxos.com

length, he seems to speak of his own inner loneliness with an immediacy that can make the listener feel almost intrusive.

Not long before he wrote the "Razumovsky" Quartets, Beethoven had experienced his third rebuff by a woman whom he had hoped to marry. At this point in his life he seems to have liked to keep it all within the family, as it were—their family, not his. Having lost one countess, Giulietta, he now fell in love with another, her cousin Josephine. Still later, he would fall in love with her sister Therese.

Josephine, forced into an unhappy marriage but recently widowed, had suffered a nervous breakdown following the birth of her fourth child. At around this time she also started having piano lessons with Beethoven, whose chivalrous instincts quickly developed into an intense romantic passion. Whether she ever actively reciprocated his feelings we shall probably never know. But from a characteristically clumsy letter explaining his recent state of mind, there seems no doubt that he believed she did (the underlinings are Beethoven's):

*Josephine von
Brunsvik*

It is true that I haven't been as active as I should have been—but a great <u>inner</u> <u>unhappiness</u> deprived me of my usual buoyancy, ever since my feelings of love for you, O desirable J., began to spring up within me, and this increased further. When we are together, undisturbed, then you shall be told all about my real suffering and of the struggle which has gone on within me for some time between life and death. A fact which for a long time made me doubt whether there can really be any happiness at all in <u>life on this earth</u>—now it is not half so desperate—for I have won your heart!... My *activity will increase once again—and this I promise you by all I hold highest and most precious, in a short time I will be there, <u>worthier of myself and of yourself</u>. Oh, if only you would be willing to establish my happiness through your love—to increase it. Oh, my beloved, it is not a desire for the opposite sex which draws me to you. No, you, <u>your whole self</u>, with all your characteristics, have fettered all my feelings, my entire sensitivity, to you....You overwhelmed me, whether you did it willingly or unwillingly. O Heavens, let our love endure for a long, long time... It is noble—based so much on mutual respect and friend-ship—indeed the very similarities in so <u>many</u> things—in thinking and feeling. Oh let me hope that your heart will long beat for me. <u>Mine</u> can only cease beating for you when it <u>no longer beats at all</u>. O my <u>beloved</u>, keep well! But I also hope that you may be happy <u>through me</u>. Other-wise I would be—<u>selfish</u>.*

Love letters seldom bring out the best in their writers, linguis-tically speaking, but Beethoven's letters to Josephine show him at his most inarticulate. No one was more aware than he that words were not his strong point, but in the case of these partic-ular letters the inarticulate sometimes borders on the incoher-ent:

Oh why is there no language which can express what is far above all mere regard—far above everything—that we can never describe—Oh, who can name you—and not feel that however much he could speak about you—that would never attain—to you—only in music—Alas, am I not too proud when I believe that music is more at my command than words— You, you, my all, my happiness—alas, no—even in my music I cannot do so, although in this respect thou, Nature, hast not stinted me with thy gifts. Yet there is too little for you. Beat, thou, in silence, poor heart—that is all you can do, nothing more—for you—always for you— only you—eternally you—only you until I sink into the grave—my refreshment—my all. Oh, Creator, watch over her—bless her days—

rather let all calamities fall on me—Only you—Even if you had not fettered me again to life, yet you would have meant everything to me.

And what were Josephine's feelings for the man who wrote these heartfelt outpourings? Her affection and admiration are beyond doubt. If an undated letter, presumed to have been written at roughly the same time, suggests a certain confusion of mind on her part, its overall message seems unambiguous:

My own spirit, which was enthusiastic for you before we had ever met, received nourishment from your inclination. A feeling which lies deep within my heart and is not capable of expression, made me love you. Before I met you, your music made me enthusiastic for you—the goodness of your character, your inclination towards me increased my enthusiasm—this prerogative which you granted me, the pleasure of being with you, could have been the greatest jewel of my life—if you loved me less sensually. Because I cannot satisfy this sensual love you are angry with me—but I would have to destroy sacred bonds if I were to give heed to your desires. Believe me that the fulfillment of my duties causes me the greatest suffering—and that the motives which guide my conduct are noble.

This letter is not entirely convincing. The "sacred bonds" she mentions concern a vow of chastity she claimed to have taken on her unloved husband's death. But such a vow seems unlikely in the light of what we know about her character and conduct both before and after; and her apparently chaste discomfort with Beethoven's sensuality can hardly be as straightforward as she makes it sound. It is clear from the diaries of Therese that both sisters were given to bouts of promiscuity in which Josephine alone gave herself (Therese's words) "freely and unconcernedly." It would be nice to think that Beethoven was unaware of this.

As relations gradually cooled between Beethoven and Josephine, his intimacy with her sister Therese steadily increased. During this period he seems at least partially to have come to terms with his deafness. On a page of sketches for the "Razumovsky" Quartets, he wrote in pencil, "Let your deafness no longer be a secret—even in art." Accordingly, he now turned out one masterpiece after another, many of them radiating a kind of triumphant serenity. Among them was the epic **Violin Concerto in D** of 1806. Seldom has a great work received a more inauspicious premiere. The soloist, one Franz Clement, apparently read the concerto at first sight, and between movements entertained the audience by playing on one string with the fiddle held upside down. But even worse premieres were to come.

"Let your deafness no longer be a secret— even in art."

In December 1808 Beethoven mounted a long-awaited concert at which he unveiled a number of his most recent works. The program took four hours and included the **Fifth** and Sixth symphonies, the **Fourth Piano Concerto**, the Fantasia ("Choral Fantasy") for piano, orchestra, soloists, and chorus, a solo improvisation by Beethoven himself, the aria *Ah! perfido* and movements from the Mass in C. In the audience was the composer, violinist, and conductor Louis Spohr:

Beethoven was playing a new concerto of his, but already at the first tutti, forgetting that he was the soloist, he jumped up and began to conduct in his own peculiar fashion. At the first big accent he threw out his arms so wide that he knocked over both lamps from the music stand of the piano. The audience laughed, and Beethoven was so beside himself over this disturbance that he stopped the orchestra and made them start again. Seyfried, worried for fear that this would happen again in the same place, took the precaution of ordering two choirboys to stand next to Beethoven and to hold the lamps in their hands.

One of them innocently stepped closer and followed the music from the piano part. But when the fatal moment burst upon us once more, the poor boy received from Beethoven's right hand such a sharp slap in the face that in sheer terror he dropped the lamp on the floor. The other, more wary boy, who had been anxiously following Beethoven's movements, succeeded in avoiding the blow by ducking in time. If the audience had laughed the first time, they now indulged in a truly Bacchanalian riot. Beethoven broke out in such a fury that when he struck the first chord of the solo he broke six strings. Every effort of the true music lovers to restore calm and attention remained unavailing for some time; thus the first Allegro *of the* Concerto *was completely lost to the audience. After this accident, Beethoven wanted to give no more concerts.*

Away from the piano, Beethoven was one of the clumsiest of men. As one eyewitness reported:

Beethoven as a conductor was little short of catastrophic.

Beethoven was most awkward, even bungling, in his behavior; his clumsy movements were entirely lacking in grace. It often seemed that he could scarcely pick anything up without dropping or breaking it. Everything in his rooms appeared to have been knocked over, soiled, or destroyed. How he ever managed to shave himself at all remains difficult to understand, even considering the frequent cuts on his cheeks. A further peculiarity is that, try as he might, he could never learn to dance in time with the music.

From this, it follows naturally that Beethoven as a conductor was little short of catastrophic. Ignaz von Seyfried has left us an unforgettable vignette:

When it came to conducting, our Beethoven could in no way be called a model, and the orchestra had to pay heed lest it be misled by its mentor, for he thought only of his tone-poems, and was ceaselessly engaged in calling attention to their authentic expression by means of manifold gesticulations. He was accustomed to indicate a diminuendo *by trying to make himself smaller and smaller, and at the* pianissimo *he would slip down under the conductor's desk, so to speak. As the tonal masses increased in volume, he too seemed to swell, as though out of a stage trapdoor, and with the entrance of the entire body of instrumental tone he would rise up onto the very tips of his toes, until swaying in the air with his arms, he seemed to be trying to float up into the clouds. He was all active movement, no organic part of him was idle, and the whole man might be compared to a* perpetuum mobile. *When he observed that the players were entering into his intentions and playing together with increasing ardor, inspired by the magical power of his creations, his face would be transfigured with joy.*

Given the tragedies of his personal life, it can be easy to overlook the fact that joy is not only a central feature of Beethoven's music, but perhaps even the dominant one. Indeed, this transcendent joy is one of the lynchpins of his enduring reputation as the greatest composer who ever lived.

Interlude III:
Beethoven and the Human Voice

Beethoven's vocal works form the least-known branch of his output. Most of them today are completely unfamiliar to all but connoisseurs. Yet he wrote nearly 100 original songs, many more settings of folksongs, forty canons, five cantatas, one oratorio, two masses, and some miscellaneous pieces for chorus or smaller vocal ensembles. What is more, he was an innovator.

Music for Solo Voice

As a songwriter, Beethoven inherited little in the way of tradition. There were, of course, fine German songs before his, including a number by Haydn and Mozart. But the emergence of the German Lied as a major art form occurred during Beethoven's lifetime, and he did much to lay the foundations for its development. The story of Lieder is often said to begin with Schubert; but the fact is that most of Beethoven's songs were composed before any of Schubert's. It is one of musical history's greatest ironies that Beethoven and Schubert lived and worked in the same not-very-large city for all but a year of Schubert's life without ever having met. Beethoven, indeed, was scarcely aware of his younger contemporary. Only on his deathbed did he come to know any of Schubert's songs, and he was reportedly greatly moved and excited by them. Only one of Beethoven's individual songs has found lasting fame, and that an early one: *Adelaide*, an Italianate love song written in 1795, under the influence of Salieri. Composed in a *bel canto* style that he was soon to desert, the song is remarkable, among other things, for the variety of moods, shades and meanings in which he manages to clothe the reiterated name of the singer's beloved, Adelaide (pronounced Ah-de-lah-eeda).

Beethoven's greatest contribution to the history of the Lied, however, is not a single song but a song-cycle, *An die ferne Geliebte* ("To the Distant Beloved"), Op. 98. Today the term song-cycle immediately evokes the great examples by Schubert and Schumann; but *An die ferne Geliebte*, while not the first, may be seen as the foundation stone. What distinguishes a song-cycle from a mere collection of songs is a unifying theme, usually either a narrative thread, external or internal, or an overall mood. Cycles are also frequently built around a carefully chosen sequence of keys. In most of the songs of his immediate predecessors, including Mozart, the emphasis tends to be on a folklike simplicity, with the piano as a junior partner. Often, the right-hand part duplicates the singer's melody, while the left provides a basic harmonic backdrop. The text is usually little more than a convenient moodsetter, and illustrative tone-painting is rare. Beethoven gave a high priority to both quality and expressive content in his choice of texts, and was almost obsessive in his matching of musical rhythm with that of the words. In all these respects, *An die ferne Geliebte* was seminal. Never before had a composer taken such pains to bind contrasting songs into a coherent and unified whole. Indeed, with its linking piano interludes and recall of the opening song at the end, *An die ferne Geliebte* is more truly "cyclic" than the song-cycles of Schubert.

> Beethoven gave a high priority to both quality and expressive content in his choice of texts, and was almost obsessive in his matching of musical rhythm with that of the words.

Beethoven's numerous folksong settings are variable, but the best are very fine indeed and their almost wholesale neglect is a shame. They were begun in 1809 at the request of the Scottish publisher George Thomson, who had already enlisted Pleyel, Kozeluch, and Haydn in the cause. They exist in several forms for various numbers of singers, though most are solo songs with piano accompaniments augmented by optional parts for violin and cello. In addition to the many Scottish, Welsh, and Irish tunes (these all commissioned by Thomson), Beethoven extended his geographical net to incorporate folksongs from Portugal, Spain, Italy, Russia, Sweden, Poland, Ukraine, Hungary, and Switzerland. These Thomson refused to publish, so Beethoven found homes for them elsewhere.

The young Beethoven's grasp of choral and orchestral possibilities was remarkable.

Music for Chorus

Beethoven's cantatas began on a grandiose scale. The *Cantata on the Death of Joseph II* and its companion piece on the accession of Leopold II to the imperial throne, both composed in 1790, were designed for special occasions that clearly fired the nineteen-year-old's imagination. Indeed, Beethoven thought highly enough of the "Joseph" Cantata in later years to adopt from it a movement for **Fidelio**, his only opera. The young Beethoven's grasp of choral and orchestral possibilities was remarkable. In the opening chorus of the "Joseph" Cantata, the weeping phrases in the orchestra, the antiphonal effects between chorus and orchestra where the voices enter ejaculating the word "Tod," and the sudden dramatic *fortissimo* outburst are wonderful early instances of Beethoven's emotional power. The massive final chorus of the "Leopold" Cantata looks forward to the finale of Beethoven's **Ninth Symphony**.

CD 1
track 8

www.naxos.com

CD 2
track 8

www.naxos.com

Years later, in 1814, Beethoven's cantata *Der glorreiche Augenblick* ("The Glorious Moment"), written for the Congress of Vienna, was performed for an audience of sovereigns and princes assembled to celebrate Napoleon's defeat—an audience almost unparalleled in social brilliance. Indeed in this case, alas, the brilliance of the audience exceeded that of the cantata, which was hamstrung by an inferior text and a score matched in bombast only by *Wellingtons Sieg* ("Wellington's Victory," usually known as the "Battle" Symphony) of the same year.

The cantata *Meeresstille und glückliche Fahrt* ("Calm Sea and Prosperous Voyage") is another matter altogether. Composed in 1815 for four-part chorus and orchestra, it combines two poems by Goethe. This was because, as Beethoven explained to the poet when sending him the dedication, "Both, owing to the contrast which they offer, seem to me most fitting to be expressed musically. And how thankful I should be to know whether my harmonies are in unison with yours." Goethe, characteristically, never replied. In its way the work is a minor masterpiece, not least in the vividness and sensitivity of Beethoven's word-setting and instrumental coloring. The vocal writing is entirely idiomatic, showing no sign of the technical challenges that singers were later to complain of in the **Ninth Symphony** and the **Missa solemnis**. Much of the orchestral writing, too, is inspired, not least in the long, hypnotic *pianissimo* of the opening, in which the sun glints on the surface of the quiet sea.

With the exception of the Ninth Symphony's finale, which is a case apart, and the closely related "Choral Fantasy," Op. 80 (ditto), the major choral works of Beethoven's maturity are an oratorio and two masses. *Christus am Oelberge* ("Christ on the Mount of Olives") was written in the aftermath of the Heiligenstadt crisis of 1802, with Haydn's two great oratorios *The Creation* and *The Seasons* still fresh in Viennese minds. Essentially a dramatic meditation on the theme of universal suffering, it enjoyed great popularity in the nineteenth century, but has since largely fallen from favor. Present-day performances are rare. The Mass in C of 1807 has fared better, but has inevitably been overshadowed by the later and greater *Missa solemnis*. Beethoven described both works as being "especially close to my heart" and was not best pleased to have the C major dismissed by Prince Nikolaus Esterházy, who commissioned it, as "unbearably ridiculous and detestable." Posterity has left the prince in an ignominious minority.

Beethoven's original handwritten manuscript of the Missa solemnis, *"Dona nobis pacem"*

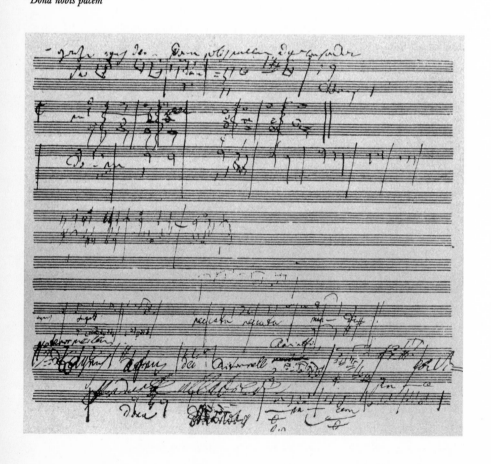

The ***Missa solemnis***, begun in 1819, had a protracted birth and was not completed until 1823. Beethoven believed it to be his greatest work, and nine generations of music lovers have tended to endorse his judgement. While originally conceived for liturgical purposes (to celebrate the enthronement of the Archduke Rudolph as Archbishop of Olmütz in 1820) and inspired by profound religious feelings, the work is of a grandeur and universality hardly containable by even the most lavish ecclesiastical ritual. With Bach's Mass in B minor it stands as one of the towering twin peaks in the whole history of the genre: a mass, yes, but one of symphonic proportions and symphonic conception. Only an intellect of gigantic stature could have conceived a work of such complexity and mastery. Yet in his famous inscription at the head of the Kyrie Beethoven says all that he wishes to say, all that need be said: "From the heart—may it go to the heart!" This is a transcendently emotional work, with a transcendently spiritual purpose. "My chief aim, when composing this grand Mass," he wrote, "was to awaken and permanently instill religious feelings not only into the singers but also into the listeners." His success is a matter of historical record.

CD 2
track 5

www.naxos.com

Chapter 4

The Immortal Beloved

The Immortal Beloved

At the time of his marathon concert in 1808, Beethoven, not yet forty, was probably the most popular and certainly the most widely known composer in the world. But no revolutionary is universally loved. To many conservatives, in fact, Beethoven was a monster, a wilfully destructive menace to the noble traditions of Mozart and Haydn. Their presumption could be breathtaking. Take the eminent dramatist August von Kotzebue, writing in the Viennese journal *Die Freimütige*:

> *All impartial musicians and music lovers are agreed that there was never anything so incoherent, shrill, chaotic, and earsplitting as Beethoven's music. The most piercing dissonances clash in a truly atrocious harmony, and a few puny ideas only increase the disagreeable and deafening effect.*

The groundswell of what Moscheles described as "Beethoven fever" swept right across the Habsburg Empire, particularly amongst the younger generation. No serious composer enjoyed better sales, no composer of such comparative youth appeared so regularly on concert programs. Yet he seems to have been consumed with financial anxiety and fears for his immediate future. "Sometimes," he wrote to a friend, "I feel that I shall soon go mad in consequence of my unmerited fame. Fortune is seeking me out and for that very reason I almost dread some fresh calamity." But none came, at least not yet. In 1809 his financial worries were laid to rest when the Archduke Rudolph, along with the Princes Kinsky and Lobkowitz, settled on him a comfortable annuity designed to keep him in Vienna. Characteristically ready to look a gift horse in the mouth, however, Beethoven was prepared to haggle, insisting on a number of conditions of his own, without which he would not be prepared to accept the offer. In the event he withdrew most of them, having satisfied his sense of pride, and the definitive document was drawn up and signed on March 1:

Prince Lobkowitz,
(1772–1816),
one of Beethoven's
generous patrons

AGREEMENT:

The daily proofs which Herr Ludwig van Beethoven is giving of his extraordinary talents and genius as musician and composer, awaken the desire that he surpass the great expectations which are justified by his past achievements.

But as it has been demonstrated that only one who is as free from care as possible can devote himself to a single department of activity and create works of magnitude which are exalted and which ennoble art, the undersigned have decided to place Herr Ludwig van Beethoven in a position where the necessaries of life shall not cause him embarrassment or clog his powerful genius.

To this end they bind themselves to pay him the fixed sum of 4,000 (four thousand) florins a year, as follows:

73

His Imperial Highness, Archduke Rudolph . . . . *Fl. 1,500*

The Highborn Prince Lobkowitz *700*

The Highborn Prince Ferdinand Kinsky *1,800*

Total . . . . *Fl. 4,000*

which Herr van Beethoven is to collect in semiannual installments, pro rata, against voucher, from each of these contributors.

The undersigned are pledged to pay this annual salary until Herr van Beethoven receives an appointment which shall yield him the equivalent of the above sum.

Should such an appointment not be received and Herr Ludwig van Beethoven be prevented from practicing his art by an unfortunate accident or old age, the participants herein grant him the salary for life.

In consideration of this Herr Ludwig van Beethoven pledges himself to make his domicile in Vienna, where the makers of this document live, or in a city in one of the other hereditary countries of His Austrian Imperial Majesty, and to depart from this domicile only for such set times as may be called for by his business or the interests of art, touching which, however, the high contributors must be consulted and to which they must give their consent.

Given in Vienna, March 1, 1809

(L.S.) Rudolph, Archduke.

(L.S.) Prince von Lobkowitz, Duke of Raudnitz.

(L.S.) Ferdinand Prince Kinsky.

Significantly, each of the signatories was Beethoven's junior. At thirty-five, Lobkowitz was the eldest, while Kinsky and Rudolph were twenty-seven and twenty-one respectively. It was significant because of Beethoven's particular appeal to the young. Certainly none of the three got better value for his money than Rudolph, who was obviously an exceptional pianist. He was eventually to be the dedicatee not only of the famous **"Archduke" Trio, Op. 97** (see p. 201) but also of the magnificent E flat Piano Concerto known in English-speaking countries as the "Emperor" (ironically, in view of the "Eroica" episode), the "Lebewohl" Sonata ("Les Adieux"), Op. 81a, the "Hammerklavier" Sonata, Op. 106, and the *Missa solemnis.*

Beethoven is widely held to be the most universal of all composers. Through the power of his vision and the sheer force of his personality his music seems to have unlocked areas of feeling that listeners worldwide have recognized as common to all humanity. The greatness of his music lies beyond the power of analysis to explain, but it can be amply demonstrated by the testimony of listeners from all walks of life through two centuries. Apart from anything else, it is music of towering strength. Among the many things that make Beethoven's music unique is its extraordinary capacity to inspire courage. More than that, it has led many people to experience, at the highest level, a sense of community that far transcends the comforts simply of company. Nor does one need any knowledge of his life and circumstances to feel this. In some ultimately mysterious way, he makes us feel, through his example, that we can confront reality without fear. The key word here, of course, is "feel." We don't actually *lose* our fears, any more than he did. Fear, after all, is as much a part of life as suffering and the capacity for joy, both of that Beethoven had in abundance. What is so uniquely life-enhancing about Beethoven is his *response* to fear, not his lack of it. Closely related to this, and equally important, is his attitude to suffering.

By the standards of our modern industrial societies, with their in-built materialism, Beethoven's views were distinctly

> Among the many things that make Beethoven's music unique is its extraordinary capacity to inspire courage.

old-fashioned. Today, perhaps particularly in the West, there is a widespread tendency to regard suffering as an undesirable, and potentially curable, manifestation of life. For Beethoven, it was neither undesirable nor avoidable. It was a fact of life, and his changing attitudes to it, from childhood to death, form the central drama of his life, and, by extension, of his music. In childhood, as in the later crisis over his hearing, his first response was to withdraw. But this was never a mere withdrawing *from*. It was a withdrawal *into* a world of imagination and fantasy where he could roam undisturbed, and where he was in control. In this sense, it was no withdrawal at all but an *entry* into resources and regions of the mind that often remain closed to the rest of us. He escaped *into* music.

For Beethoven, suffering was neither undesirable nor avoidable.

In matters of sexual or romantic love (or rather its frustration or withdrawal), his normal practice was to plunge himself into unremitting hard work. The response to his encroaching deafness was more complicated. His immediate instinct, as evidenced by the "Heiligenstadt Testament," was to retreat into a kind of tormented isolation.

I must withdraw from everything. And my best years will rapidly pass away without my being able to achieve all that my talent and my strength have commanded me to do. Indeed I shall be cut off from everything that is most dear to me.

And in this first phase, we find something very like shame. He reveals his plight to two friends only, both far removed from Vienna, and enjoins them to secrecy: "I implore you to keep what I have told you about my hearing in the strictest confidence, to be entrusted to no one, whoever he may be." But retreat was never really his game. The first unmistakably positive response, perhaps predictably, was defiance. "I will take

Fate by the throat!" he famously declared—and take it by the throat he did. In the famous **Fifth Symphony**, Fate, to use Schindler's imagery (not Beethoven's, as generally believed), is heard to knock menacingly at the door. No sooner is it across the threshold, however, than it gets the trouncing of its life; and the symphony ends with a fantastic, joyful celebration of triumph over adversity.

The heroic courage of Beethoven's response is endlessly exciting, but Fate—or the inevitability of suffering, call it what we may—is too fundamental an adversary to be dealt with even by Beethoven's once-beloved "morality of power." It was not enough to rebel against it, however heroically. Rebellion could no more alter the facts than it could be indefinitely maintained. As with most conflicts, the solution lay in a coming to terms, which naturally required time, and involved a measure of contradiction. "Many times have I cursed my Creator and my own existence," Beethoven wrote, in 1801. "But Plutarch has shown me the path of resignation....Resignation!...What a wretched resource! Yet it sometimes seems that this is all that is left to me." Later, resignation was replaced by something less passive, something that required an act of will, even if the desired end was still a form of retreat. But to judge from some of the strangely disjointed entries in his journal, his mind was still in some confusion:

> *Submission, absolute submission to your fate, only this can give you the sacrifice...to the servitude—oh, hard struggle!—Turn everything which remains to be done to planning the long journey—you must yourself find all that your most blessed wish can offer, you must force it to your will—keep always of the same mind....O God, give me the strength to conquer—myself!*

What he came to understand, and what can be heard with overpowering clarity when you study his music, is that suffering is not something external but an essential part of human experience. Before he could transcend it, it was necessary for Beethoven to accept it, to embrace it, even, as a part of his own wholeness. The organic unity of his greatest music—its psychological and emotional unity—is something that is instinctively felt by people all over the world, people who may not know the first thing about sonata structure or key relations or the history of the scherzo. And its message, whether Beethoven intended one or not, is of hope, and of a triumphant faith in the power of human resilience.

In addition to his worsening deafness and his chronic abdominal problems, which often left him in a good deal of pain, Beethoven continued to be unlucky in love. In 1810, after rebuffs from two countesses with whom he may or may not have had an affair, he was refused in his proposal of marriage to the young niece of his doctor. Therese Malfatti was a mere eighteen years of age, and the thought of being married to this swarthy, rough-mannered little man (already reputed in some circles to be half-mad) was clearly not for her, genius or no genius. One can see her point. As Anton Schindler makes plain, Beethoven's outer aspect at this point in his life inspired a modicum of caution:

Beethoven could not have been much more than five feet four inches tall. His body was thick-set, with large bones and a strong muscular system; his head was unusually large, covered with long, unkempt, almost completely grey hair, giving him a somewhat savage aspect, enhanced even more when his beard had grown to an immoderate length, which was quite often the case. His forehead was high and broad, his brown eyes small, almost retreating into his head when he laughed. They could, however, suddenly become unusually prominent and large, either rolling and flashing—the pupils almost always turned upwards—or not moving at all, staring fixedly ahead when one idea or another took hold of him. When that happened, his whole appearance would suddenly and conspicuously alter, with such a noticeably inspired and imposing look that his small figure would loom before one as gigantically as his spirit. These moments of sudden inspiration often befell him in even the most jovial company, but also in the street, which generally attracted the close attention of passersby. His mouth was well formed, the lips not quite even, the lower predominating somewhat, the nose rather broad. With his smile a most benevolent and amiable air spread over his whole face; this was of special benefit when he conversed with strangers, for it encouraged them. His laughter, on the other hand, often burst out immoderately, distorting the intelligent and strongly marked features; the huge head was wont to swell, the face would become still broader, and the whole effect was often that of a grimacing caricature.

In the aftermath of his rejection by Therese Malfatti, Beethoven, as usual in such situations, threw himself into a bout of intensive hard work, and much of the music he wrote reflects the white heat of his creative fire. In the catalogue of Beethoven's relations with women, however, one name stands out from all the others—or rather the *absence* of her name does. Among the papers discovered in his belongings after his death was a very long, three-part letter to a woman he addressed as his "Immortal Beloved" without ever naming her. As with the mysterious "dark lady" of Shakespeare's sonnets, her identity has posed one of the greatest puzzles in the history of biography. Several names, and many theories, have been put forward, of which one, and perhaps only one, seems entirely convincing. In his 1977 biography of Beethoven, the American scholar Maynard Solomon identifies her as Antonie Brentano, the wife of one of Beethoven's most constant and valued friends. But this time it seems to be Beethoven drawing back at

"His laughter, on the other hand, often burst out immoderately, distorting the intelligent and strongly marked features."

The beginning of Beethoven's letter to his "Immortal Beloved" the critical moment—Beethoven, whose craving for a wife and family had been at times almost an obsession. No one familiar with Beethoven's letters, and this letter in particular, can doubt the sincerity of the anguish and confusion expressed here. More elusive is its meaning:

July 6, in the morning.

My angel, my all, my very self—Only a few words today and at that with pencil (with yours)—Not till tomorrow will my lodgings be definitely determined upon—What a useless waste of time—Why this deep sorrow when necessity speaks—can our love endure except through sacrifices, through not demanding everything from one another; can you change the fact that you are not wholly mine, I not wholly thine—Oh God, look out into the beauties of nature and comfort your heart with that which must be—Love demands everything and that very justly—thus it is to me with you, and to you with me. But you forget so easily that I must live for me and for you; if we were wholly united you would feel the pain of it as little as I—My journey was a fearful one; I did not reach here until four o'clock yesterday morning. Lacking horses the post-coach chose another route, but what an awful one; at the stage before the last I was warned not to travel at night; I was made fearful of a forest, but that only made me the more eager—and I was wrong. The coach must needs break down on the wretched road, a bottomless mud road. Without such postilions as I had with me I should have remained stuck in the road. Esterházy, traveling the usual road here, had the same fate with eight horses that I had with four—Yet I got some pleasure out of it, as I always do when I successfully overcome difficulties—Now a quick change to things internal from things external. We shall surely see each other soon; moreover, today I cannot share with you the thoughts I have had during these last few days touching my own life—If our hearts were always close together, I would have none of these. My heart is full of so many things to say to you—ah—there are moments when I feel that speech amounts to nothing at all—Cheer up—remain my true, my only treasure, my all as I am yours. The gods must send us the rest, what for us must and shall be.

Your faithful LUDWIG
Evening, Monday, July 6.
You are suffering, my dearest creature—only now have I learned that letters must be posted very early in the morning on Mondays and Thursdays—the only days on which the mail-coach goes from here to K.—You are suffering—Ah, wherever I am, there you are also—I will arrange it with you and me that I can live with you.

At this point, Beethoven abruptly changes gear and embarks on a passage of metaphysical musing that at times is almost incoherent, suggesting a considerable confusion of mind:

What a life!!! thus!!! without you—pursued by the goodness of mankind hither and thither—which I as little want to deserve as I deserve it—Humility of man towards man—it pains me—and when I consider myself in relation to the universe, what am I and what is He—whom we call the greatest—and yet—herein lies the divine in man—I weep when I reflect that you will probably not receive the first report from me until Saturday—Much as you love me—I love you more—But do not ever conceal yourself from me—good night—As I am taking the baths I must go to bed—Oh God—so near! so far! Is not our love truly a heavenly structure, and also as firm as the vault of heaven?

The third part of the letter seems to have been written almost as soon as he opened his eyes on awakening:

Good morning, on July 7.
Though still in bed, my thoughts go out to You, my Immortal Beloved,

now and then joyfully, then sadly, waiting to learn whether or not fate will hear us—I can live only wholly with you or not at all—Yes, I am resolved to wander so long away from you until I can fly to your arms and say that I am really at home with you, and can send my soul enwrapped in you into the land of spirits—Yes, unhappily it must be so—You will be the more contained since you know my fidelity to you. No one else can ever possess my heart never—never—Oh God, why must one be parted from one whom one so loves. And yet my life in Vienna is now a wretched life—Your love makes me at once the happiest and the unhappiest of men—At my age I need a steady, quiet life—can that be so in our connection? My angel, I have just been told that the mail-coach goes every day—therefore I must close at once so that you may receive the letter at once.—Be calm, only by a calm consideration of our existence can we achieve our purpose to live together—Be calm—love me—today yesterday—what tearful longings for you—you—you my life—my all—farewell.—Oh continue to love me never misjudge the most faithful heart of your beloved.

Ever thine
ever mine   *L.*
ever ours

The letter was clearly never sent, nor does it contain any hint as to where it was written. Indeed its obscurities as regards the woman's identity show every sign of having been deliberate. The only geographical pointer is disguised by an initial, "K." There is no reference to her marital status, let alone to parenthood. From the tone of the letter it appears virtually certain that she reciprocated his love for her and was prepared to make great sacrifices to enter into union with him.

There can be no doubt that this affair caused Beethoven far more pain than his rejection by Therese Malfatti. But there is one other possibility, and that is that the whole thing is an elaborate fantasy–that the Immortal Beloved is not *a* woman but Woman; that she represents the sum total of Beethoven's hopes, desires, and fears of women generally, and marriage in particular. There is another interesting point here. The letter has been convincingly traced to the summer of 1812, yet it has no musical counterpart. In the G major Violin Sonata, Op. 96, composed in the immediate aftermath of the letter, Beethoven the titanic wrestler gives way to a particular kind of gentleness and serenity. It is as though this crisis, at least, had finally been resolved, and left him with a newly clarified and comforting sense of his *own* identity.

In that same summer of 1812, Beethoven travelled to the Bohemian spa town of Teplitz, where he met the only comparable giant of contemporary German culture, the poet, playwright, and polymath Johann Wolfgang von Goethe. Beethoven had long admired Goethe's poetry. His several Goethe-inspired works had culminated, two years earlier, in his incidental music for the drama *Egmont.* Not long after their meeting in Teplitz he began a setting of Goethe's *Meeresstille und glückliche Fahrt,* which he dedicated to the poet, noting in a letter that "the admiration, the love and esteem which already in my youth I cherished for the one and only immortal Goethe have persisted." This was despite a measure of disillusionment with the man himself. Though the two had been daily companions for a time during their stay in Teplitz, each had been disappointed in the other. "Goethe," wrote Beethoven, "is too fond of the atmosphere of the royal courts, more than is becoming to a poet. Why laugh at the absurdities of virtuosos when poets, who ought to be the first teachers of a nation, forget everything for the sake of glitter?"

Goethe for his part confided his impression of Beethoven to his friend, the composer and teacher Carl Friedrich Zelter:

A more self-contained, energetic, sincere artist I never saw. His talent amazed me. Unfortunately he is an utterly untamed personality, who is not altogether in the wrong in holding the world to be detestable, but does not make it any the more enjoyable, either for himself or others, by his attitude. He is very excusable, on the other hand, and much to be pitied, as his hearing is leaving him.

There were few things that Beethoven loathed more than to be pitied. Some might say, uncharitably, that his self-pity left little room for the pity of others. There are numerous instances where he describes himself to friends as "God's most unhappy and miserable creature" and so on. In his journal, too, he frequently invokes the Almighty. "God help me. Thou seest me forsaken by all Mankind. O harsh fate, O cruel destiny! No, no—my miserable state will never end!"

To the world at large, however, and in his relations with individuals encountered in day-to-day affairs, he could present a very different face from the "untamed personality" described by Goethe. Among those taking the waters at the Bohemian spa was Karl von Ense:

> Some might say, uncharitably, that his self-pity left little room for the pity of others.

In that summer at Teplitz, I made Beethoven's acquaintance and found this allegedly wild and unsociable man to be the most magnificent artist with a heart of gold, a glorious spirit and a friendly disposition. What he has refused to princes he granted to us at first sight—he played for us on the piano. I was soon on intimate terms with him, and his noble character, the uninterrupted flow of a godlike spirit which I always seemed to feel with an almost reverential awe when in his very silent presence, drew me closely to him, to such an extent that day after day I did not ever feel the burden of his company, which, on account of his deafness, most people found rather exhausting.

Unlike many composers, Beethoven was quite ready to talk about his method of composing, which gives a fascinating insight into the workings of his mind:

> *I carry my ideas about with me for a long time, often for a very long time, before I write them down. In doing so, my memory is so trustworthy that I am sure I will not forget, even after a period of years, a theme I have once committed to memory. I change a great deal, eliminate much and begin again, until I am satisfied with the result; then the working-out, in extension, in diminution, in height and in depth begins in my head, and since I know what I want, the basic idea never leaves me, it mounts and grows, I hear and see the work in my mind in its full proportions, as though already accomplished, and all that remains is the labor of writing it out; this proceeds quickly, depending on the time I have available, since I often have several pieces in the works at once; I am certain, however, not to confuse one with another. If you ask me where I get my ideas, that I cannot say with any certainty. They generally come unbidden, indirectly, directly. I could grasp them with my hands; in the midst of nature, in the woods, on walks, in the silence of the night, in the early morning, inspired by moods that translate themselves into words for the poet and into tones for me, that sound, surge, roar, until at last they stand before me as notes.*

Anton Schindler, chronicler of Beethoven's life

Anton Schindler has proved to be a somewhat unreliable chronicler of Beethoven's life and conversation; but there is no reason to suspect the following account of his work habits:

> *Beethoven rose at daybreak, no matter what the season, and went at once to his work-table. There*

he worked until two or three o'clock, when he took his midday meal. In the interim he usually ran out into the open two or three times, where he also "worked while walking." Such excursions seldom exceeded a full hour's time, and resembled the swarming out of the bee to gather honey. They never varied with the seasons and neither cold nor heat were noticed. The afternoons were dedicated to regular promenades; and at a later hour Beethoven was wont to hunt up some favorite beer-house, in order to read the news of the day, if he had not already satisfied this need at some café.

Ignaz von Seyfried recalled in florid style a delightful incident that occurred in 1801:

Every year Beethoven spent the summer months in the country, where under skies of azure blue he liked best to compose, and composed most successfully. Once he took lodgings in romantic Mödling, in order to be able to enjoy the Lower Austrian Switzerland, the picturesque Brühl, to his heart's content. So a four-horse wagon was freighted with a few articles of furniture and a tremendous load of music; the tower-like machine slowly got underway, and the owner of its treasures marched along ahead of it as happy as could be. No sooner did he cross the city boundary and find himself among blossoming fields, where gentle zephyrs set the green corn swaying like waves amid the jubilant song of fluttering larks, celebrating the longed-for coming of lovely spring with trills of raptured greeting, than his genius awoke; thoughts began to traverse his mind, were spun out, ranged in order, noted down in lead pencil—and the aim and goal of his migration was entirely forgotten. The gods alone know whither our Master strayed during the whole long period which elapsed, but suffice to say it was not until dusk was falling that dripping with sweat, covered with dust, hungry, thirsty, and tired to death, he arrived in his chosen Tusculum. Yet, heaven be merciful, what a horrible spectacle awaited him there! The driver had made his snail-like way to his destination without misadventure, but had waited two full hours for the patron who had hired and already had paid him in advance. Since he did not know his patron's name it was impossible to make inquiries; and in any event the cart-horse tamer wished to sleep at home. So he had made short work of it, unloaded the entire contents of his wagon in the marketplace and drove off without further ado. Beethoven was at first very angry; then he broke into uproarious laughter. After a brief pause for reflection, he hired half-a-dozen gaping street boys, and had all he could do before the cries of the watchmen announcing the midnight hour rang out on the air, to get the children of his brain safely under the shelter of a roof by the light of Luna's silver ray.

Few men were quicker to anger than Beethoven; fewer still were quicker to repent. This cycle was among his most exasperating and endearing features. In a volatile lifetime he alienated many, and hurt many more. But he rarely lost a friend.

Interlude IV:
Beethoven and the Orchestra

The Symphonies

Ask the average music lover to name the five most famous symphonies ever written and the chances are that the reply will include four by Beethoven: the **"Eroica" (No. 3)**, the **Fifth** (with its memorable "fate knocking at the door" motif), the "Pastoral" (No. 6), and the **"Choral" (No. 9)**. Nowhere more so than in his nine symphonies did Beethoven take his courtly eighteenth-century heritage and transform it into a blazing celebration of individual liberty and the triumphant power of the human spirit. There is scarcely a corner of our emotional, spiritual, and psychological experience that does not somewhere, somehow, find transcendent expression in Beethoven's music. And each of his symphonies marks a particular stage of his own spiritual development.

The fact that he delayed embarking on his **First Symphony** until 1799, his twenty-ninth year, is significant. His youth and early manhood are documented by a varied output of piano

CD 1
track 5
www.naxos.com

CD 2
track 2
www.naxos.com

CD 2
track 8
www.naxos.com

CD 1
track 3
www.naxos.com

He begins by "blowing a raspberry," in the form of a lone, two-chord cadence.

sonatas, concertos, chamber music, choral music, and so on, many of which reveal a downright boisterous self-confidence. From an early age, he felt a powerful sense of destiny, quickened by a brashly competitive streak. He knew full well that when he tackled the symphony he must be brave enough, and sufficiently well-armed, to confront the awesome examples of Mozart and Haydn head-on. With the very opening gesture of his First Symphony he not only declares himself ready but openly mocks the expectations of his audience. He begins by "blowing a raspberry," in the form of a lone, two-chord cadence—the standard combination for ending a piece, not beginning one. Not only does he start with a stop, as it were, he does it in the wrong key. Three bars later he is still in cadential mode and still in the "wrong" key, but now a different one. For many at the time, this was an outrage, precisely as Beethoven intended. At the start of the last movement he plays out the notes of an ascending scale one by one, each new step arousing a different degree of expectation. Bashful he wasn't. No composer, not even Haydn, ever got more artistic mileage out of the frustration of expectation than Beethoven.

In the Second Symphony (1801–2) he uses similar devices but this time on an altogether bigger scale. In the third movement he takes note that his title "Scherzo" is the Italian word for joke and makes a big show of obsessive repetition—though admittedly on nothing like the scale he was later to adopt in the "Pastoral" Symphony. His major surprise, however is in the final movement. Everything about the symphony so far has suggested (or would have done to the audiences of his time) that Beethoven is conforming to the pattern of Haydn's late symphonies by following two extensive movements with two relatively brief ones. But just when we expect him to be winding up for the close, he goes sailing into a riotously inventive coda (literally, "tailpiece") that eventually accounts for a third of the movement.

With the Third Symphony, the **"Eroica"** (1803), we come to one of the most revolutionary works in the history of art. Here the expansionism evident in the finale of the **Second Symphony** is extended to the entire work, which is half as long again as any symphony then written. The music's physical scale and emotional range are vast, its demands on the players unprecedented. In addition to its epic reach, much of the detail along the way is of a complexity and originality for which no one was prepared. If the Second represented the swansong of the Classical symphonic ideal as perfected by Haydn and Mozart, the Third may be said to have ushered in a new age.

For some reason, Beethoven's odd-numbered symphonies have always enjoyed greater popularity than the even-numbered ones, the major exception being No. 6, the "Pastoral." This is particularly a shame in the case of No. 4 (1806), perhaps the least often heard. Shorter and more economical in the number of its notes than the "Eroica," it demonstrates as well as anything that in Beethoven the sense of "space" is not dependent on length. The mood of the work as a whole is strikingly different from the prevailing heroism of the Third, but its intensity is comparable and its vitality just as irresistible, if less forceful. Broadly speaking, Beethoven's themes fall into two categories. On the one hand there are the beautiful, long-spun melodies such as those in the Fourth Symphony, especially its glorious *Adagio*; on the other there are short, motto-like figures that can hardly be described as melodies at all.

A perfect case in point is the opening of the famous **Fifth Symphony**, completed in 1808. "Thus does Fate knock at the door," Beethoven is reported to have said. Dot–dot–dot–DASH–silence–Dot–dot–dot–DASH: this is

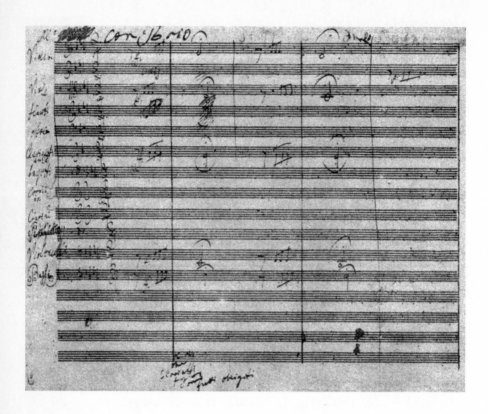

Opening bars of Beethoven's Fifth Symphony, original manuscript

a theme, yes; a tune, no. But from such acorns do Beethovenian oaks often grow. A remarkable amount of the first movement derives directly from this characteristically terse idea, and its rhythm later plays an important part in the scherzo and finale. It also haunts a number of Beethoven's other works—sometimes in similarly "fateful" mode, as in the first movement of the "Appassionata" Sonata; but often to very different effect, as in the first movement of the lyrical **Fourth Piano Concerto**. For edge-of-the-seat excitement and adventure in music, the Fifth Symphony takes the palm. As millions of listeners have discovered over two centuries, one needs no musical "knowledge" whatever to recognize in this work the triumph of the will over adversity. Starting with all the trappings of tragedy, it is one of the most overpoweringly positive works ever conceived; and the weird, shifting, shadowy transition from the scherzo to the finale, with its sense of hovering between life and death, is among the most original passages in all music. Only in the triumphant finale does Beethoven unleash his full orchestral forces, including trombones and piccolo. Having begun the work with a standard Classical orchestra, as used by Mozart and Haydn, he ends with a triumphal hymn to the new spirit of Romanticism that was to dominate the nineteenth century.

CD 2
track 2

www.naxos.com

The **Fifth Symphony** and the Sixth, the so-called "Pastoral" (1808), are as different as two siblings can be; yet they were completed in rapid succession and premiered at the same concert. Where the Fifth was the most dynamic and densely packed symphony ever written, the Sixth was the most expansive and relaxed. In many ways it was also the most unconventional. Alone among Beethoven's symphonies, it has five movements, of which the last three are played without a break. It is and yet is not (in both cases according to the composer) "program music," just as it is and is not (again according to the composer) replete with "tone-painting." The title "Pastoral" is Beethoven's own, as is the subtitle, "Recollections of Country Life." But he qualifies this by adding "more the expression of feeling than tone-painting." Each of the movements bears a heading:

1. *Awakening of Cheerful Feelings upon Arriving in the Countryside*
2. *Scene by the Brook*
3. *Merry Gathering of Country Folk*
4. *Thunderstorm*
5. *Shepherd's Song–Happy and Thankful Feelings after the Storm*

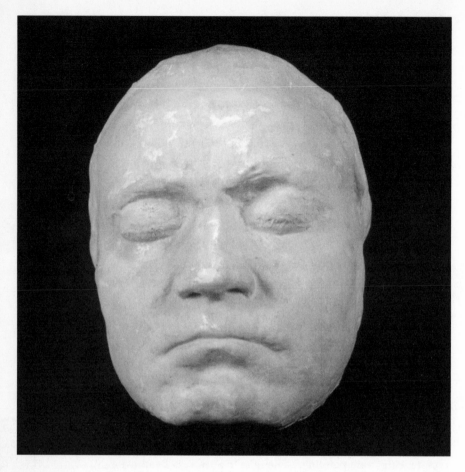

Face mask of Beethoven made in 1812 while he was working on his Seventh Symphony. Mould made by Franz Klein

Second in length only to the "Eroica," this was the most leisurely symphony yet written, often relying for its effect on daringly inspired repetition. One passage in the first movement, for instance, holds the same unchanging harmony for more than a dozen bars.

After the music itself, the most famous thing about the **Seventh Symphony** (1811–12) is Wagner's characterization of it as "the apotheosis of the dance." Certainly no symphony thus far (and that includes the Fifth) is more rhythm-based than this one, in which each movement derives its greatest unity from obsessive repetition and development of certain basic rhythmic patterns. Like the Eighth, this is also a symphony with no real slow movement: in place of the expected *Adagio* or *Andante* Beethoven wrote a haunting, marchlike A minor *Allegretto* that had to be encored at early performances. The only slow section is the imposingly spacious introduction to the first movement, which characteristically sows many of the seeds that come to fruition in the movement proper.

The Eighth Symphony (1812) is more compact, and its good humor abundant and contagious. Its chief significance in historical terms lies in its structure, both in the layout of its movements and within the movements themselves. As in the Seventh, there is no real slow movement. Instead, a comical, scherzo-like *Allegretto* is followed by a leisurely, courtly minuet that looks back nostalgically to the eighteenth century. There is comedy of a more explosive, anarchic sort in the finale, whose coda—huge even by Beethoven's standards—contains what are in effect a second development and a second recapitulation.

After the Eighth, Beethoven abandoned the medium of the symphony for a dozen years. When he returned to it in 1822–4, it was with a work even more colossal in scale and revolutionary in procedure than the "Eroica." The **Ninth Symphony** would have secured an important place in history even without its groundbreaking choral finale (a setting of Schiller's *Ode to Joy*). But while much of the work was radically innovative, it is rooted in the Classical symphonic ideal. Beethoven still uses sonata form as the principal agent of dramatic movement; he still includes a scherzo (itself in full sonata form); and he still uses the opposition and eventual reconciliation of different keys as a major structural and expressive device. But he does it all on such a huge aural canvas, and with such an awe-inspiring emotional and intellectual power, that one feels like an eavesdropper at the creation of the universe.

CD 2
track 8
www.naxos.com

Among the symphony's many unique features (the most obvious of which is the use of soloists and chorus) is the fact that the massive finale contains within it not only the framework of sonata form but also that of an entire Classical four-movement symphony. More, perhaps, than any other single work, the Ninth Symphony opened the floodgates of Romanticism, and became an object of near-obsession with such powerfully individual figures as Wagner and Berlioz.

The Concertos

Beethoven's seven mature concerto examples form the core of the concerto repertoire as we know it today: the five piano concertos, the **D major Violin Concerto**, and the "Triple Concerto" for piano, violin, and cello. Of the piano concertos, the first two were composed during Beethoven's early years in Vienna, but published in reverse order of their composition. No. 1 in C, Op. 15 (written in 1795 and probably revised in 1800) postdates **No. 2 in B flat, Op. 19**, which was begun before 1793 (possibly as early as 1788), completed in the winter of 1794–5 and revised in 1798. Both works find Beethoven in Mozartian vein; and both reveal his gift for long-spun, highly expressive melodies and his irrepressible sense of humor, which ranges from high wit to a deliberately heavy-handed jokiness. But while Mozart may be their stylistic godfather, the personality behind them is unmistakably Beethoven's. Both works are virtuoso vehicles, of considerably greater technical difficulty than most of Mozart's concertos; and the uniquely long cadenza in the first movement of the C major, probably composed later, around 1809, gives us a hint of what Beethoven's fabled improvisations must have been like.

Though not without its Mozartian debts, the Third Piano Concerto in C minor, Op. 37, begun in 1800 but not completed until 1803, is considerably darker and more emphatically Beethovenian, with its "fate-tinged" opening theme, its unusual key relations and its sustained intensity. The first movement is altogether more dramatic, with the solo part taking full advantage of the recently expanded compass of the piano. The extremely slow *Largo* central movement is in the remote, luminous key of E major and inhabits a new and uniquely Beethovenian realm of rarefied feeling.

In the **Fourth Piano Concerto in G, Op. 58** (1804–6), Beethoven made history by beginning with a phrase played, unaccompanied, by the soloist before the orchestra is heard (though Mozart had come close to this in his E flat Concerto, K.271). The answer from the orchestra, in a completely different key, is not only surprising but one of the most magical moments in all music. The whole work has a spaciousness and serenity that make it, for many, the most beautiful concerto ever written. The only significant clouds in this heavenly landscape come in the slow movement: a dramatic dialogue between a glowering, fate-laden orchestra and the unaccompanied piano—calming, lyrical, and infinitely wise. In the other movements, as in Mozart's concertos, the integration of soloist and orchestra—so far from the gladiatorial, rigged combat of the standard Romantic concerto—enhances the broadly symphonic feel of the work as a whole.

> The whole work has a spaciousness and serenity that make it, for many, the most beautiful concerto ever written.

The same can be said of the Fifth Piano Concerto in E flat, Op. 73 of 1809, known in English-speaking countries as the "Emperor," though here the soloist is grandly heroic as well as being the agent of rapt poetry. After a single call-to-arms by the orchestra, Beethoven reverses tradition by *beginning* the work with an extended and virtuosic cadenza for the piano before giving out the noble main theme in the orchestra. In grandeur, tenderness, magic, and excitement, the work remains

unsurpassed; and although it sounds as if it is the most difficult for the soloist of all Beethoven's piano concertos, it is in fact the least difficult to play.

Strange to say, it took almost forty years for Beethoven's sublime **Violin Concerto, Op. 61**, to gain full acceptance by audiences. The main problem seems to have been the unprecedented length of the first movement. Another factor may have been the fact that while it is by no means easy to play, Beethoven never indulges in idle bravura display. In that respect, audiences reared on the virtuoso vehicles that gained popularity in the wake of Paganini (the "demon fiddler") may well have felt themselves shortchanged. No major work by Beethoven is so radiant in its serene self-confidence and lyrical impulse.

The neglected child among Beethoven's concertos, relatively speaking, is the Concerto for piano, violin, cello, and orchestra, Op. 56 (the "Triple Concerto"), written in 1804–7. It is something of a transitional work, and Beethoven's only experiment with multiple soloists. Treating them both as a trio and as individuals, he gives primacy not to the piano, as might be expected, but to the cello, writing predominantly in its eloquent higher register. A big, sometimes sprawling work, it is perhaps the most uneven of the concertos, but its rewards heavily outnumber its drawbacks.

> Beethoven never indulges in idle bravura display.

Chapter 5

Kidnapped

Kidnapped

In the waning months of 1812, Beethoven's fortunes took a sharp downward turn. In addition to his physical afflictions and his luckless love life, he was once again, and against all expectations, in financial difficulties. Almost from the outset, the triple annuity that had been designed to free him of material want had run into trouble. As he complained, well over a year after its signature, "Kinsky has not yet paid me a farthing." By the end of the year, Kinsky had died in a riding accident and Lobkowitz had gone bankrupt, his payments consequently being frozen. Of the three signatories, only the Archduke Rudolph had kept his word. In the meantime, Austria's financial crisis, exacerbated by Napoleon's visit, had deepened to the point where the florin was officially devalued fivefold. Beethoven's promised 4,000 florins had dwindled overnight to a mere 800. His music, too, was taking him ever further into uncharted waters.

As foreshadowed in the **"Razumovsky"** Quartets, Beethoven was entering a phase of composition whose challenges proved too much for concert audiences—too difficult, indeed, even for some of his colleagues. Apart from a few sympathetic and influential aristocrats, he effectively lost much of his public. Unsurprisingly, he now fell into a deep depression that brought his creative energies to their lowest ebb. Such sexual energies as survived in him were spent joylessly in brothels and were succeeded by a sense of guilt and bouts of self-loathing that only intensified his inner loneliness. For more than a year he composed almost nothing of consequence, and his friends were alarmed to find him in what some of them described as a "deplorable condition"—so unkempt and unhygienic that guests in various inns and taverns went out of their way to avoid sitting anywhere near him. As the Baron de Trémont discovered, a visit to Beethoven's lodgings only confirmed the impression:

> *Picture to yourself the extreme of dirt and disorder, pools of water decorating the floor, and a rather ancient grand piano on which dust competed for room with sheets of written or printed notes. Under it— I do not exaggerate—an unemptied chamber pot; beside it, a small walnut table accustomed to the frequent overturnings of the secretary placed upon it; a quantity of pens encrusted with ink, compared with which the proverbial tavern-pens would shine; and then more music. Most of the chairs had straw seats and were decorated with clothes and with dishes full of the remains of the previous day's supper.*

As far as his Viennese audience was concerned, Beethoven looked like he was becoming a forgotten man. But not for long. In the autumn of 1813, he was sought out by the German inventor Johann Mälzel, who two years later was to introduce the metronome. One of his more extravagant inventions was an extraordinary contraption that he called the Panharmonicon, an entirely mechanical orchestra-substitute for which he hoped Beethoven would write a grandiose piece of program music depicting the Duke of Wellington's victory over Napoleon in the Battle of Victoria. Beethoven obliged, and while he was about it he made a conventionally

Beethoven looked like he was becoming a forgotten man.

101

Portrait of Beethoven at the piano by Hermann Junker

orchestrated version for more normal performance. In the virtually unanimous judgement of posterity, *Wellingtons Sieg*, commonly known as the "Battle" Symphony, is the worst piece of music Beethoven ever wrote.

Posterity may not have liked it, but it caused a sensation in Vienna. It had four spectacular performances in quick succession, and the composer once again became a local hero. Happily, this ironic change in Beethoven's fortunes paved the way for Vienna's acceptance of his most recent genuine symphonies, the **Seventh** and the Eighth, and brought in a lot of much-needed money. Far the most important result, from Beethoven's point of view, however, was the successful staging of his only opera, **Fidelio**, which he had now thoroughly revised after two earlier, unsuccessful productions (see page 121).

In the aftermath of this unexpected upturn in his fortunes, Beethoven, by now predictably, changed his address. As Seyfried wrote:

> *One of Beethoven's curious manias was his passion for changing his lodgings—although moving with all his possessions always greatly discommoded him, and was invariably accompanied by a loss of belongings. No sooner had he taken possession of a new dwelling-place than he would find something objectionable about it, and then would run his feet sore trying to discover another. As a result it sometimes happened that he rented various lodgings at the same time.*

And generally this was at a cost he had failed to calculate. Among the most surprising of his shortcomings was his apparent failure to master basic arithmetic. He could add but not multiply, even at comparatively low levels. If asked for the product of four times fifteen, he would laboriously write out "15 + 15 + 15 + 15," arriving at the answer in three separate stages. His numerous landlords and their tenants were usually, though not invariably, glad to see the back of him. Ironically, as Schindler reported, it was often because of the sounds he made:

> *Beethoven especially liked seating himself at the piano in the twilight and improvising, and often he also played the violin or viola, which instruments always lay ready to hand for this purpose on the piano-top. How this playing sounded, since his outer senses no longer could participate in it, it is needless to say; particularly in the case of the string instruments, which he was unable to tune. His playing must have been torture to the ears of those who lived in the same house.*

But there was more. Despite the material squalor of his various apartments, Beethoven, against the odds, was addicted to personal hygiene:

"His playing must have been torture to the ears of those who lived in the same house."

> *Washing and bathing were among the most indispensable necessities of existence for Beethoven. In this respect he was a thorough Oriental. If, while he was working, he did not go out during the morning, in order to compose himself he would stand at the wash-basin, often minimally attired, and pour great jugfuls of water over his hands, at the same time howling or, for a change, growling out the whole gamut of the scale, ascending and descending; then, before long, he would pace the room, his eyes rolling or fixed in a stare, jot down a few notes and again return to his water pouring and howling. These were moments of profoundest meditation, nothing worth making a great fuss about had they not resulted in disagreeable consequences in two directions. In the first place, they often incited his servants to laughter, observing which the Master would fly into a rage. Or he would get into a fight with the landlord when the water leaked through the floor which, unfortunately, often happened. This was a principal reason why Beethoven was everywhere unwelcome as a lodger.*

In 1814 he made his last public appearance as a pianist. At the age of forty-three his hearing had deteriorated so far that, according to Spohr:

There was scarcely anything left of the virtuosity which had formerly been so greatly admired. In the strongest passages, the poor man pounded on the keys till the strings jangled, and in the quieter ones he played so softly that whole groups of notes were omitted, so that the music was quite unintelligible.

The end of his performing career was a melancholy, if predictable, milestone in Beethoven's professional life. Far more significant, though, was an event that took place some eighteen months later. On November 15, 1815, Beethoven's brother Caspar Carl died, leaving behind him a hornet's nest of family tensions that eventually led to an attempted suicide and nearly cost Beethoven his sanity.

Beethoven had never approved of his brother's wife Johanna, who gave birth to a boy, Karl, less than four months after the wedding. From the beginning, the marriage was an unhappy one, leading at one point to a public denunciation in which Caspar Carl accused his wife of embezzling money. The fact that the money was actually hers to begin with—a part of the dowry she had brought to the marriage—was overlooked, and she was convicted and sentenced to a month's house arrest. This event was to play a significant role in a three-way tragedy largely precipitated by Beethoven himself.

In his dying days, Caspar Carl specified in his will that the guardianship of the boy was to be shared by Johanna and Beethoven. By means never divulged, Beethoven persuaded him to redraft the will, leaving the mother out altogether and entrusting the boy's care and education entirely to Beethoven. At first, he complied; but within a matter of hours he thought better of it and wrote a codicil to the will that made his original intentions unequivocally clear:

> *Having learned that my brother, Ludwig van Beethoven, desires after my death to take wholly to himself my son Karl, and wholly to withdraw him from the supervision and training of his mother, and inasmuch as the best of harmony does not exist between my brother and my wife, I have found it necessary to add to my will that I* by no means *desire that my son be taken away from his mother, but that he shall always and so long as his future career permits remain with his mother, to which end the guardianship of him is to be exercised by her as well as my brother. Only by unity can the object which I had in view in appointing my brother guardian of my son be attained, wherefore, for the welfare of my child, I* recommend compliance to my wife and more moderation *to my brother. God permit them to be harmonious for the sake of the child's welfare. This is the last wish of the dying husband and brother.*

Less than a day later he was dead.

From that moment onwards, Beethoven lost no opportunity to blacken Johanna's name, habitually referring to her as "the Queen of the Night," after the villainess of Mozart's opera *The Magic Flute.* He devoted most of his energies to proving her legally, morally, and intellectually unfit to have any say in the boy's upbringing. In effect he was seeking the legal sanction of a kidnapping. Naturally he brought up her conviction for embezzlement; he also managed to convince himself, and the lawyers, that she was little better than a common whore. "Last night," he reported, "the "Queen of the Night" was at the Artist's Ball until three in the morning, exposing not only her mental but also *her bodily nakedness*–it was whispered that she–was willing to hire herself–for 20 gulden! Oh most horrible!"

He devoted most of his energies to proving her legally, morally, and intellectually unfit to have any say in the boy's upbringing.

In fact there was no justification for the claim, any more than there was for his obsessive suspicion that she had poisoned her husband. He likewise had fantasies that she was having him watched, that she was bribing his servants. In his own mind, he was engaged on a sacred quest: to "rescue" the hapless child from the forces of evil, just as Leonore in *Fidelio* rescues her unjustly imprisoned husband from the clutches of the wicked Pizarro. He bolstered his determination with strange exhortations in his journal. "Ignore all gossip," he wrote to himself, "...all gossip, and all pettiness, for the sake of this holy cause. These circumstances are very hard for you, but He who is above exists. Without Him there is nothing. In any case, the token has been accepted." The nature of the token goes unexplained.

Within two months of his brother's death, and in direct contradiction of his last wishes, Beethoven actually succeeded in his campaign to gain sole legal charge of the boy. Accordingly, on February 2, 1816, the nine-year-old Karl was forcibly taken from his mother and ensconced by his uncle in a private school for boys. Beethoven and the headmaster Giannatasio del Rio then appealed to the court for an injunction banning all communication between the boy and his mother. Two days later Beethoven wrote to a friend in terms of jubilation: "I have fought a battle for the purpose of wresting a poor, unhappy child from the clutches of his unworthy mother, and I have won the day! *Te Deum laudamus!!!*"

Needless to say, the "poor, unhappy child" had not been consulted. But, as Beethoven was soon to discover, the case was far from over. Whatever else may be said of her, Karl's mother was no pushover. She too went to court, repeatedly, and for the next five years the boy became a human shuttlecock and the subject of endless litigation between two strong-minded adults, neither of whom was cut out for the role of parenthood but only one of whom could truly call him by the name of son. To begin with, even Beethoven granted that.

Along with his several paranoid fantasies about Johanna, however, went another, that put their relationship, and his relationship to Karl, into a new and unexpected light. In May 1816 he wrote unassumingly to a friend: "I now regard myself as Karl's father." Four months later it was no longer a matter of self-regard. As he bluntly, and disturbingly, put it in another letter, "I am now the real, *physical* father of my dead brother's child."

The implications of this bizarre delusion seem not to have troubled him. For the moment, it only fanned the flames of his hostility to her. His letters, his journal, his conversations are a furnace stoked by innumerable unjustified accusations and bitter attacks on Johanna's character. Karl was continuously indoctrinated against his mother and roundly applauded whenever he contributed a few missiles of his own to the relentless barrage of slanders directed at her. When Beethoven belatedly discovered that mother and son had several times contrived to meet in secret, he was predictably enraged:

> "As I often give him a good shaking, but never without valid reason, he was far too frightened to confess everything."

> I had been noticing signs of treachery for a very long time; and then one day I received an anonymous letter the contents of which filled me with terror; but they were little more than suppositions. Karl, whom I pounced on that very evening, immediately disclosed a little, but not all. As I often give him a good shaking, but never without valid reason, he was far too frightened to confess everything. But the servants, who had often witnessed me chastising him, overheard us—and that old traitress, my housekeeper, actually *tried* to prevent him from confessing the truth! But everything came to light. Karl has done wrong, but one must grant that a mother—even a bad mother—is still a mother... Everything here is in a state of great confusion. Still, it won't be necessary to take me to the madhouse.

Perhaps not. But increasing numbers of people, and not just those who knew him, began to believe that Beethoven was indeed going mad. Again, there is no reason to mistrust Schindler's account:

Beethoven's outward appearance, due to his quite peculiar neglect in the matter of dress, had something uncommonly conspicuous about it in the street. Usually lost in thought, and humming to himself, he often gesticulated with his arms when walking by himself. When in company, he would speak quite animatedly and loudly, and since his companion then had to write his rejoinder in the conversation book, an abrupt halt would have to be made; this was conspicuous in itself, and was still more so when the rejoinder was communicated in mime. And so it happened that most of the passersby would turn around to stare at him; the street urchins also made their gibes and shouted after him. For that reason, his nephew Karl refused to go out with him and once told him straight out that he was ashamed to accompany him in the street because of his "comical appearance." The double lorgnette, which he wore for his shortsightedness, hung loose. The coattails were rather heavily laden: apart from a pocket handkerchief, which often showed, they contained a thick, folded quarto music notebook and a conversation book with a thick carpenter's pencil, for communicating with friends and acquaintances he might happen to meet; and at an earlier period, so long as it was of any use, an ear-trumpet. The weight of the music notebook lengthened one coattail considerably, and the pocket was often turned inside out when the notebook and conversation book were extracted from it.

It was not only on the street that his sanity was questioned. His conduct indoors, as Ries reports, could be positively alarming:

Beethoven was sometimes extremely violent. One day we were dining at the Swan; the waiter brought him the wrong dish. Beethoven had scarcely said a few choice words about it, which the waiter had answered perhaps not quite as politely as he might have, when Beethoven laid hold of the dish—a kind of roast beef with lots of sauce— and flung it at the waiter's head. The poor fellow still had on his arm a large number of plates containing various dishes (a dexterity which Viennese waiters possess to a high degree) and could do nothing to help himself; the sauce ran down his face. He and Beethoven shouted and cursed at each other, while all the other guests laughed out loud. Finally Beethoven too began laughing at the sight of the waiter, who lapped up with his tongue the sauce that was dribbling down his face, tried to go on hurling insults, but had to go on lapping instead, pulling the most ludicrous faces the while—a picture truly worthy of Hogarth.

Beethoven's violence, like almost every other aspect of his life and character, was a powerful and revolutionary part of his music too. The number of sudden, stabbing accents in his music was unprecedented. No composer before him ever made such a feature of disruptive contrasts between loud and soft. It follows that no other composer was better suited to the depiction of storms. The one that blows up in his "Pastoral" Symphony is a sensational case in point.

As we know, violence was one of the facts of life with which Beethoven grew up. But his father was not the only perpetrator. He was regularly beaten and abused by his schoolmasters too, at least one of whom was notorious for the savagery of his punishments, often for the most trivial offenses. Just as many child abusers today were themselves abused children, so Beethoven quite readily allowed, even occasionally encouraged, Karl's teachers to beat him into obedience. But the physical punishment meted out to Karl was trivial in comparison with the psychological suffering he was made to endure. One of the reasons for Beethoven's rage after discovering the secret meetings of Karl and his mother was not merely the disobedience but the fact that his own attempts to keep them apart had failed. Very early on in his guardianship he wrote to Karl's headmaster:

> *It will certainly be best to remove the boy from Vienna as soon as possible and send him to some place where he will neither see nor hear anything more of his beastly mother, and where everything about him is strange. That way, he will have fewer people to lean upon and will have to win love and respect by his own efforts alone.*

Yet while planning to send this already troubled nine-year-old to a foreign city, he was still able to write in his journal:

> *What is a boarding school compared with the immediate sympathetic care of a father for his child? A thousand beautiful moments vanish when children are in wooden institutions, whereas at home, with good parents, they could be receiving impressions full of deep feeling, which endure into the most extreme old age.*

He was hardly speaking from experience. If pressed, he could probably not have come up with even a hundred such moments from his own childhood. Two closely related self-images dominated Beethoven's life, both of them justified, and both of them abused. On the one hand he saw himself as a victim, on the other as a hero—usually a hero on *behalf* of life's victims. And it often seemed that the one was needed to fuel the other, as though he had a vested interest in being misunderstood or cheated, even when there was no evidence for either. Heroism requires an adversary. If none presents itself, then it must be manufactured:

> *Oh, I am a man harried on all sides like a wild beast, misunderstood, and often treated in the basest way! I, who am saddled with so many*

cares, with the constant battle against this monster of a mother, who always attempted to stifle good. She has continually induced my beloved Karl to dissimulate, to bribe my servants, to tell lies. She has even given him money in order to arouse lusts and desires which are harmful to him. Under her care he became completely perverted and was encouraged to deceive his own father. I confess that I myself am better fitted than anyone else to inspire my nephew by my own example with a desire for virtue and zealous activity.

This juxtaposition of self-pity and self-congratulation runs through Beethoven's letters and journals like twin tributaries. His actions and attitudes often followed suit, veering from one extreme to the other with a suddenness that must have been as bewildering to him as to those around him. There was no consistency even in his behavior towards Johanna. At one moment he would do everything in his power to prevent all contact between mother and son; at the next he would be cooperative, sometimes almost friendly, taking her himself to see Karl at school, or arranging meetings at his lodgings. The continuous alternation between vindictiveness and a sense of natural justice can only have sent the most confusing signals to Karl, not least when Beethoven presumed to speak for both of them as one. Johanna, on the other hand, would have read between the lines just as Beethoven intended:

Alas, our many occupations made it quite impossible for Karl and I to send you our best wishes on New Year's Day. But I know that without this explanation you are fully assured of both my own and Karl's wishes for your welfare. As for your need of money, I would gladly have helped you out with a sum. But unfortunately I have too many expenses and debts...so that I cannot prove to you at once and on the spot my readiness to help you. Meanwhile I assure you now in writing that henceforth and forever you may draw Karl's half of your pension... Both Karl and I wish you all possible happiness.

At the time he undoubtedly meant it. It seems clear that he did sometimes feel doubts about his actions, which he then did his best to justify to himself in his journal. Whether he still felt that he stood closer to God than most people, it was to God that he frequently addressed himself, often in a state of some confusion:

> *I have done my part, O Lord! It might have been possible without offending the widow, but it was not. Only Thou, Almighty God, canst see into my heart, knowest that I have sacrificed my very best for the sake of my dear Karl. Bless my work! Bless the widow! Why cannot I obey all the prompting of my heart and help the widow? God, God! My refuge, my rock, O my all! Thou seest my innermost thoughts and knowest how it pains me to be obliged to compel others to suffer by my good labors for my precious Karl!!!*

But the "precious Karl," too, was often the victim of his uncle's mood swings. When he once ran away to rejoin Johanna, Beethoven's reaction was swift and categorical. "Karl is unloving, ungrateful, and callous. He is most fit for the company of his own mother and my *pseudo-brother*. Nay, he is a monster. My love for him is gone. *He needed my love.* I do not need his!" Yet in the very same letter he adds, "You understand, of course, that this is not what I *really* think. I still love him as I used to, *but without weakness.* In truth, I often weep for him." He wept with good reason. His conversation books, where his companions and associates wrote rather than spoke their own contributions, contain pages of the most pathetic entries from Karl, and some of considerable courage:

"Karl is unloving, ungrateful, and callous. He is most fit for the company of his own mother and my *pseudo-brother*. Nay, he is a monster."

> *I beg of you once more not to torment me as you are doing; you may come to regret it, for I can stand much but too much I cannot endure.*

You treated your brother the same way today with no reason. You must remember that other people are human too.

Will you let me go out for a little today? I need recreation. I will come back later.

I only want to go to my room.

I am not going out, I only want to be alone for a little.

Won't you please let me go to my room?

It could reasonably be suggested that in "weeping for Karl" Beethoven was actually weeping for himself. There were certainly times when he seems to have rued the day he ever embarked on his supposed rescue mission; when he seemed to hold Karl responsible, as though Karl were imprisoning *him*:

God is my witness, I dream only of getting completely away from you and from this wretched brother and that horrible family which has been thrust upon me. May God grant my wishes, for I can no longer trust you... Unfortunately your father—or, better still, not your father...

And what was the poor boy supposed to make of that? This from the man who had effectively stolen him from his own mother, expressly against the dying wishes of his father. True to form, Beethoven would later be overcome with remorse and would beg for forgiveness. It was the pattern of almost every friendship or relationship he ever had. According to his own testimony there were only two friends in his life whom he had not succeeded in alienating, and each of them, not coincidentally, lived far away and communicated almost exclusively by letter.

When not being abusive, both physically and verbally, Beethoven frequently used his well-exercised self-pity as an agent of emotional blackmail. During one summer when he was taking the waters at Baden, Karl, now nineteen and a student at the Polytechnic Institute in Vienna, was expected to visit him every Sunday. He failed to do so. Beethoven's response was to try to inspire guilt for his (as he saw it) unwarranted neglect. He wrote to Karl:

> Beethoven would later be overcome with remorse and would beg for forgiveness. It was the pattern of almost every friendship or relationship he ever had.

I am getting thinner and thinner, and am ailing rather than well. I have no doctor, not a single sympathetic soul at hand. If you can come to visit me on Sunday, please do. But I don't want to interfere in your plans....It seems I must learn to give up everything....oh! where have I not been wounded, nay more, cut to the heart!

Such melodramatic overplaying was counterproductive. Karl's impulse was to stay away. But when Beethoven heard that he had been seeing his mother again, he changed tack. He now threatened to provoke a showdown, forcing Karl to choose between his mother and his uncle, or rather his self-styled "father." "If the bond is to be broken," he wrote, "so be it. But you will be detested by all impartial people when they hear of your ingratitude." This, of course, they would only do from Beethoven himself, and there is no evidence that he was keen to publicize the matter. As usual after his more emotional outbursts, he was soon overcome by regret, and did all he could to repair the damage as soon as possible:

Not a word more, my dearest Karl. Not one word more…Only come to my arms. You won't hear a single hard word. For God's sake do not abandon yourself to misery. You will be welcomed here as affectionately as ever. We will lovingly discuss what has to be considered and what must be done for the future. On my word of honor you shall hear no reproaches, since in any case they would do no good. All that you may expect from me is the most loving care and help—only come, come to the faithful heart of your father, Beethoven.

The faithful heart? Beethoven may have believed that. It seems improbable that Karl did.

By 1820 Beethoven's love affair with Vienna and the Viennese had long since become a thing of the past. Dr Karl von Bursy met him only once, and was surprised to find him so voluble on the subject:

He told me a lot about his life and about Vienna. He was venomous and embittered. He raged about everything, and is dissatisfied with everything, and he curses Austria, and Vienna in particular. He speaks quickly and with great vivacity. He often banged his fist on the piano, and made such a noise that it echoed around the room. He is not exactly reserved; for he told me much about his personal affairs and related much about himself and his family. He complains about the present age, and for many reasons. Art, he says, no longer occupies a position high above the commonplace, and is no longer held in such high esteem and particularly not as regards recompense. Beethoven complains of bad times in a pecuniary sense. Can one believe that such a giant can have grounds for such complaints?! "Why, then," I asked him, "do you remain in Vienna when every foreign potentate would be glad to give you a place at his court or next to his throne?" "There are certain conditions that keep me here," he replied, "but everything here is mean and dirty. Things could hardly be worse. From top to bottom, everything here is shabby. You can't trust anyone. What is not written down in black and white, no one will honor. They want your work and then pay you a beggar's pittance, not even what they at first agreed to pay."

Beethoven had now largely withdrawn from society. His health steadily declined, and when he did venture out for any length of time, he was given to loud and heated diatribes against the city and those who governed it. It says much for the esteem in which he was held by the Viennese in general, and for his reputation for extreme, if harmless, eccentricity, that the police in Metternich's Vienna were prepared to look the other way. But then, as the travelling Englishman Sir John Russell makes plain, he hardly looked like a dangerous enemy of the state:

> *The neglect of his person gives him a quite wild appearance. His hair, which neither comb nor scissors seem to have visited for years, overshadows his broad brow in a quantity and confusion to which only the snakes round a Gorgon's head offer a parallel. His general behavior accords with the unpromising exterior. Except when he is with his chosen friends, kindliness or affability are not his characteristics. The loss of his hearing has deprived him of all the pleasure which society can give and perhaps soured his temper. He used to frequent a particular tavern, where he spent the evening in a corner, beyond the reach of all the chattering and disputation of a public room, drinking wine and beer, eating cheese and red herrings, and studying the newspapers. One evening a person took a seat near him whose countenance did not please him. He looked hard at the stranger, and spat on the floor as if he had seen a toad, then glanced at the newspaper, then again at the intruder, and spat again, his hair bristling into more shaggy ferocity, till he closed the alternation of spitting and staring, by fairly exclaiming, "What a scoundrely phizz!" and rushing out of the room.*

"He looked hard at the stranger, and spat on the floor as if he had seen a toad."

CD 2
track 5
www.naxos.com

CD 2
track 8
www.naxos.com

CD 2
track 6
www.naxos.com

Yet this was the man who at that very period was at work on the ***Missa solemnis***, the **Ninth Symphony**, and the **last of his thirty-two piano sonatas**, which seems to encapsulate in its two unique movements the whole of Beethoven's spiritual journey: from the defiant fist in the face of fate, through the almost superhuman struggle with his destiny, on to the stillness of acceptance and finally to a transfiguring serenity.

Interlude V:
Beethoven in the Theatre

The story of Beethoven and the theatre is fraught with irony. No composer's music is more dramatic, no dramatic music is more masterfully crafted; yet he wrote only one full-length opera. Beethoven spent three of his formative years (1789–92) playing the viola in an opera orchestra, yet showed no interest in writing for the stage. No man's music is less tentative; yet the road to finality in **Fidelio** was lit by a sequence of false dawns. The only theatre music he composed during his Bonn years was for a historical ballet organized by his patron Count Waldstein with fellow aristocrats. It did not even bear his name. The score was evidently passed off as the work of the Count himself, which may explain the surprising lack of adventurousness in its harmonies and key scheme (of its eight movements, all but one are in D major). The ballet is significant, however, as Beethoven's first purely orchestral work.

For most of his first decade in Vienna (1792–1802), Beethoven showed little interest in the stage. Apart from his studies with Salieri in Italian dramatic declamation, and two arias written for insertion into another man's opera (Umlauf's *Die schöne Schusterin*), there is nothing but the soprano aria *Ah! perfido* to suggest that he had any interest in opera at all–and the aria itself was intended for concert rather than theatrical use. The first work in which he gave his full attention to the stage was

Ballet was given a very high priority in Vienna.

another ballet, *The Creatures of Prometheus*, commissioned in 1800 by Salvatore Vigano, the famous court ballet master. Ballet was given a very high priority in Vienna. The commission of a major work like this, especially from such a source, was considered an honor for any composer. For one as inexperienced in the theatre as Beethoven, it was a very great honor indeed. Between them, Vigano and Beethoven took great liberties with the story as related by Æschylus and the Greek myths. What emerged was a mixture of the original with added elements of *Pygmalion, Orpheus,* Adam and Eve, even the Crucifixion and the Resurrection. Instead of the miscreant who stole the sacred fire from the gods, and was chained for eternity in the Caucasus, his infinitely renewable liver being eaten daily by an eagle, we get a very different tale. As related in the theatre bill, Prometheus is:

a lofty spirit, who found the men of his day in a state of ignorance and civilized them by giving them the arts and sciences. Starting from this idea, the present ballet shows us two statues brought to life and made susceptible to all the passions of human life by the power of harmony.

Act II is "placed in Parnassus and shows the apotheosis of Prometheus, who brings the men created by him to be instructed by Apollo and the Muses, thus endowing them with the blessings of culture." For Prometheus, in this case, read Beethoven (see also the quotation with which this book begins on page 2). With one exception, the Overture is the only part of the score to have achieved lasting fame.

For many, *The Creatures of Prometheus* stands as Beethoven's greatest orchestral work to date, surpassing both the first two piano concertos and the First Symphony. The theme of the finale was resurrected not once but thrice: as the seventh of the Twelve Contredanses, WoO14 (1801), as the theme of the Variations and Fugue in E flat for piano, Op. 35 (1802), and, most famously of all, as the main theme of the finale in the **"Eroica" Symphony** (1803). *Prometheus* also gives us examples of Beethoven's most picturesque scoring, notably in the use of woodwind (including the basset horn in No. 14), the prominence of the harp (very unusual for Beethoven), and the long cello solo in No. 5.

Beethoven's only finished full-length opera, *Fidelio*, had a troubled and protracted birth. Technically speaking, this is a "Singspiel," in which musical numbers alternate with spoken dialogue–other famous examples include Mozart's *The Magic Flute* (Beethoven's favorite Mozart opera) and *Die Entführung aus dem Serail* ("The Abduction from the Seraglio"). Although **Fidelio** was begun in 1804, it was not until 1814 that it reached its final form. It involves a fairly simple "rescue" story of a kind very popular in post-Revolutionary France, and for all the implausibility of the cross-dressing plot it appears to have been based on a true story. To many an inferior composer it would have been a gift. Florestan, a Spanish nobleman, has been unjustly thrown into prison by his arch-enemy Pizarro. His wife Leonore has followed him, disguised as a boy, "Fidelio," in the hope of effecting his rescue. The kindly jailer Rocco employs Fidelio, with whom his daughter Marzelline unfortunately falls in love, to the annoyance of her lover Jaquino. On learning of an imminent inspection, the tyrannical governor Pizarro decides to kill Florestan to prevent his discovery. Leonore persuades Rocco to allow the prisoners out for a while, in honor of the king's birthday. They emerge groping towards the sunlight, and gather in the open courtyard. But Florestan is not among them. He alone remains chained in the deepest dungeon, where Rocco appears with Leonore, commanded by Pizarro to dig the prisoner's grave. Pizarro tries to stab Florestan but is prevented by Leonore, who produces a small pistol. A distant trumpet heralds the arrival of the inspecting minister–an old friend, as it happens, of Florestan. The prisoners are all released; Pizarro is arrested; and Leonore herself unlocks Florestan's chains.

Beethoven became obsessed both with the deeper resonances of the plot—the theme of individual liberty versus oppression had always preoccupied him—and with the character of Leonore. For Beethoven, who craved just such a faithful and devoted wife himself, she came increasingly to represent the ideal woman. The most intriguing record of his obsession lies in his sketchbooks, where we find no fewer than sixteen sketches for the opening of Florestan's first aria alone, and a further 346 pages of sketches for the opera as a whole. The first production was on November 20, 1805, with repeat performances on the 21st and 22nd, after which it was withdrawn. Admittedly, the circumstances were far from favorable. Vienna was in French hands, the emperor and his court had fled, and the tension in the atmosphere was pervasive. Even Beethoven's most loyal supporters, however, were agreed that the opera's failure had been intrinsic, not circumstantial. Beethoven duly shortened and revised it. Four months later, it reopened, only to be withdrawn again, this time after two performances, and by Beethoven himself. Eight years were to elapse before it resurfaced, in its third, and final, version.

> The most intriguing record of his obsession lies in his sketchbooks, where we find no fewer than sixteen sketches for the opening of Florestan's first aria alone, and a further 346 pages of sketches for the opera as a whole.

What makes *Fidelio* such a transfiguring experience is neither its story nor its overtly theatrical properties (which have always been controversial) but the depth and immediacy of its underlying themes. As ever with Beethoven at his peak, the high points of the opera, and in the best sense the low ones too, far transcend their immediate context. Their ultimate power lies in the realm of pure music.

Between *Prometheus* and the final resolution of his problems with *Fidelio*, Beethoven contributed two more masterpieces to the annals of theatre music. In each case—and this was his abiding problem in the theatre—they exceeded their brief. They do not merely amplify the dramas they were intended to enhance. They overwhelm them. In the first case, this may be unsurprising. The *Coriolan* Overture (1806) was not designed for Shakespeare's tragedy *Coriolanus* but for a play on the same subject by the minor Viennese poet and playwright Heinrich von Collin (1771–1811). Beethoven's Overture, though, is worthy of Shakespeare. Its tragic power, enhanced by lyrical music of yearning beauty, preempts the spoken drama on the stage. The drama, in effect, is already complete. Even Shakespeare might have objected. Collin, on the other hand, was either too modest or too unmusical to take offense. There was talk of another "Shakespearean" double-act with Beethoven, but it came to nothing.

In the case of Goethe's *Egmont*, for which Beethoven provided not only the Overture but extensive incidental music, the playwright was not so easily dwarfed. But the Overture, like the *Coriolan* Overture, has long outlived the play in popular estimation. Both overtures are doubly miraculous. Each compresses not only the spirit but the actual course of the plot into little more than an eight-minute span. Each, too, is a musical narrative so powerful and so masterfully controlled that it has gripped the imagination of countless listeners who have no knowledge of the original story. Much of the *Egmont* incidental music is worthy of the Overture, but except for the two charming songs for Clärchen it is rarely heard–a fate it shares with Beethoven's ballets and his incidental music in general.

Beethoven's habit of overwhelming and preempting staged dramas with his overtures proved a danger even in the case of his own **Fidelio** (originally called "Leonore," his own preferred title). By the time it triumphantly reappeared in the theatre in 1814, he had written four different overtures. The discarded three are known as the *Leonore* Overtures, of which the massive, resplendent No. 3–virtually a tone-poem–is often played in the concert hall.

If Beethoven never wrote another opera, it was not for want of interest. One libretto after another was considered, covering, among other subjects, Attilla, Macbeth, Faust, Melusine, Ulysses, Bacchus, Romulus and Remus, Romeo and Juliet, Alfred the Great, and many others. The list itself tells us much about Beethoven's cast of mind and bears out what he said to Ludwig Rellstab, who tried to win him with a libretto of his own:

> *I do not mind what genre the work belongs to, so long as the material attracts me. But it must be something I can take up with sincerity and love. I could never compose operas like* Don Giovanni *and* Figaro. *Their subject matter repels me. They are too frivolous for me!*

When offered a fairy opera, *Bradamante*, he remarked: "As to magic, I am prejudiced against all that sort of thing, because it so often demands that both emotion and intellect shall be put to sleep!'

Between the music for *Egmont* and the completion of *Fidelio*, Beethoven turned his attention to two one-act Singspiels to celebrate the opening of a new theatre in Pest (not yet united with Buda). Neither *The Ruins of Athens* nor *King Stephen*, both composed in 1811, give us Beethoven anywhere near his best; and apart from sporadic performances of their overtures, they have been largely forgotten (though the "Turkish March" from the former has enjoyed considerable popularity in all manner of arrangements).

Beethoven's last work for the stage, composed in 1822, was also to mark the opening of a new theatre (or rather the re-opening of a refurbished one), the Josephstadt Theatre in Vienna. It was not, however, an entirely new conception but an adaptation of *The Ruins of Athens*, rejigged to reflect Vienna rather than Pest and renamed *The Consecration of the House*. The new Overture is a work of exhilarating splendor and Beethoven's most overt homage to Handel, whom he regarded as the greatest of all composers.

Chapter 6

The Master

The Master

As in his music, so in his life, Beethoven could often surprise. The more one studies the lives of great creative artists, the more it begins to seem that genius derives, in part, from the clash, or at least the friction, of opposites. In the case of his attitudes to the performance and publication of his works, Beethoven went to bewildering extremes. On the one hand he was a deeply principled composer of unyielding integrity, an artist, as he himself once wrote, "who prefers to hear his work performed *exactly* as it is written"; on the other, he would on occasion show an astonishing disregard for artistic principles. His colossal "Hammerklavier" Sonata, Op. 106, is arguably as great and as revolutionary as anything he ever wrote. Yet in discussion with an English publisher he seemed ready to have it chopped up any which way, like sausage meat:

> *Should this sonata not be suitable for London, I could send another one, or you could omit the* Largo *altogether and begin straight away with the Fugue, which is the last movement; or you could use the first movement and then the* Adagio, *and then for the third movement the* Scherzo—*and omit entirely No. 4—or you could just take the first movement and the Scherzo and let them form the whole sonata. I leave it to you to do as you think best.*

*Portrait of Beethoven
by H. Torggler*

This is comparable to a great writer granting his publisher permission to print the chapters of a novel in any order he liked.

It comes as no surprise, by contrast, to learn that while creating these late masterpieces, Beethoven seemed to have lost almost all touch with the practicalities of daily existence. Fortunately, he had servants to look after him. Unfortunately, he found most of them intolerable, with the result that there was a rapid turnover. One afternoon, at around four, Schindler and a friend arrived at Beethoven's lodgings to visit him:

> Beethoven seemed to have lost almost all touch with the practicalities of daily existence.

As soon as we entered we learned that in the morning both servants had left, and that there had been a quarrel after midnight which had disturbed the neighbors—both servants had gone to sleep and Beethoven found the food which they had prepared earlier inedible. In the living room, which was locked, we heard the master singing, howling, stamping. After listening to this almost terrifying performance for a long time, we were about to leave when the door opened, and Beethoven stood before us, his features so distorted that it was enough to inspire fear....His first utterances were confused, as if he had been disagreeably surprised by our overhearing him. Describing the events of the day he obviously controlled himself. "Pretty doings here," he said, "everyone has run away and I have had nothing to eat since yesterday lunch."

If absconding servants were a regular occurrence, there was a reason.

Beethoven's custom of writing down notes regarding himself, his thoughts, and his feelings also extended to details of his housekeeping. For this purpose he usually employed the blank pages of a calendar, which thus served as a kind of diary. From these we can deduce much about his record as a domestic employer. The following entries are typical and revealing:

January 31: gave housekeeper notice.

February 15: kitchen-maid entered upon her duties.

March 8: kitchen-maid gave two weeks' notice.

March 22: new housekeeper entered upon her duties.

July 20: gave housekeeper notice.

April 17: kitchen-maid entered upon her duties.

May 16: gave notice to the kitchen-maid.

May 19: new kitchen-maid left.

July 1: kitchen-maid entered upon her duties.

July 28: kitchen-maid ran away in the evening.

September 9: the girl entered service.

October 22: the girl left.

December 12: kitchen-maid entered service.

December 18: kitchen-maid gave notice.

Beethoven's approach to cuisine was highly individual; and he made exacting demands of those who prepared it. Among his favorite dishes, we learn from Seyfried,

> *was a kind of bread-soup, cooked like mush, to which he looked forward with pleasure every Thursday. Together with it, ten sizeable eggs had to be presented to him on a plate. Before they were stirred into the soup fluid he first separated and tested them by holding them against the light, then decapitated them with his own hand and anxiously sniffed them to see whether they were fresh. When fate decreed that some among them scented their straw, so to speak, the storm broke. In a voice of thunder the housekeeper was cited to court. She, however, well knowing what this meant, and between two fires, lent only half an ear to his raging and scolding, and held herself in readiness to beat a quick retreat before, as was customary, the cannonade was about to begin, and the decapitate batteries would begin to play upon her back and pour out their yellow-white, sticky intestines over her in veritable streams of lava.*

It had not always been like this. For Seyfried, it was a direct consequence of Beethoven's bodily ills:

> *The more his hearing failed, and those intestinal troubles which in the last years of his life also afflicted him gained the upper hand, the more rapidly there also developed the ominous symptoms of a torturing hypochondria. He began to complain about a world which was all evil, intent only on delusion and deceit; about malice, betrayal, and treachery. He insisted that there were no longer any honest men, saw the darkest side of everything, and at length even began to suspect his housekeeper, who had proven herself by many years of service.*

But even at the end, his misanthropy was episodic. Czerny may have oversimplified, but his basic point is echoed by virtually all Beethoven's friends:

> *Apart from those times when he was in one of those melancholy moods which occasionally overtook him, and which resulted from his physical ailments, he always was merry, mischievous, full of witticisms and jokes, and cared not a whit what people said of him.*

Always? Even the manic-depressive has his middle ground. The essence of Beethoven's greatness as a composer does not lie with the extremes of human experience, though it includes them. Rather, it lies in his ability to reflect, to relate, and to reconcile every shade of it, in a synthesis whose comprehensiveness is matched, perhaps, only by Shakespeare.

Because his manner and behavior were often so appalling, the casual reader could easily overlook Beethoven's many redeeming features: his capacity for lifelong friendships, the loyalty he inspired, his generosity to others, and the sheer pleasure that friends and acquaintances took in his company. In the words of Ferdinand Ries, "Beethoven, on the whole, was a thoroughly good and kind man, on whom his moods and impetuousness played the shabbiest of tricks." Seyfried asserts that:

> All who were better acquainted with him knew that in the art of laughter he was a virtuoso of the first rank; it was a pity, however, that even those nearest him seldom learned the why and wherefore of an explosion of the kind, since as a rule he laughed at his own secret thoughts and imaginings without condescending to explain them.

Even at his most benign, Beethoven could be a demanding friend. At one point, Seyfried tells us, he elected to solve his servant problems by demonstrating, to himself as much as to anyone else, how little he needed them:

> He suddenly decided to be quite independent, and this fantastic idea, like every other which took firm root in his mind, he proceeded at once to realize. He visited the market in person, chose, haggled over, and bought his own provisions, and undertook to prepare his own meals. This he continued to do for some little time, and when the few friends whom he still suffered about him made the most serious representations to him, he became quite angry and, as a valid proof of his own notable knowledge of the noble art of cooking, invited them to eat dinner with him the following day. There was nothing left for those invited but to appear punctually, full of expectation as to what would happen. They found their host in a short evening jacket, a stately nightcap on his bristly shock of hair, and his loins girded with a blue kitchen apron, very busily engaged at the stove. After waiting patiently for an hour and a half, while the turbulent demands of their stomachs were assuaged with increasing difficulty by cordial dialogue, the dinner was finally served. The soup recalled those charitable leavings distributed to beggars in the taverns; the beef was but half done and calculated to

"They found their host in a short evening jacket, a stately nightcap on his bristly shock of hair, and his loins girded with a blue kitchen apron, very busily engaged at the stove."

gratify only an ostrich; the vegetables floated in a mixture of water and grease; and the roast seemed to have been smoked in the chimney. Nevertheless the giver of the feast himself did full justice to every dish.

We learn more about his tastes in food and drink from Schindler:

At breakfast Beethoven drank coffee, which he usually prepared himself in a percolator. Coffee seems to have been the nourishment with which he could least dispense, and in his procedure with regard to its preparation he was as careful as the Orientals are known to be. Sixty beans to a cup was the allotment and the beans were often counted out exactly, especially when guests were present. Among his favorite dishes was macaroni with Parmesan cheese. Furthermore, all fish dishes were his special predilection. Hence guests were often invited for dinner, usually on a Friday, when a full-weight Schill (a Danube fish resembling the haddock) might be served, accompanied by complementary potatoes. For suppers on his own, he ate abstemiously. A plate of soup and some remnants of the midday meal were generally all that he took. His favorite beverage was fresh spring water which, in summer, he drank in well-nigh inordinate quantities. Among wines he preferred the Hungarian, Ofen variety. Unfortunately he liked best the adulterated wines which did great damage to his weak intestines. But warnings were of no avail in this case. Our Master also liked to drink a good glass of beer in the evening, with which he smoked a pipeful of tobacco and kept the news-sheets company. Beethoven still often visited taverns and coffeehouses in his last years, but insisted on coming in at a back door and being allowed to sit in a room apart. Strangers who wished to see him were directed thither; for he was not changeable and always chose a coffeehouse near his own dwelling. He very seldom allowed himself to be drawn into conversation with strangers presented to him in these places. When he had run through the last news-sheet he would hurriedly depart again through the back door.

"Our Master also liked to drink a good glass of beer in the evening, with which he smoked a pipeful of tobacco and kept the news-sheets company."

The early 1820s saw a marked decline in Beethoven's health. His deafness deepened and his lifelong abdominal problems became more intractable. Early in 1821 he was confined to his bed for a month and a half with what was diagnosed as rheumatic fever, and in the following summer he fell ill with jaundice. The latter was more ominous than anyone guessed at the time, leading as it did to the liver complaint that was to contribute to his death. Cirrhosis of the liver is commonly blamed on an inadequate diet and an excess of alcohol; but Beethoven's friend Karl Holz disputed that there was any question of inherited alcoholism here, pointing out, in support of his claim, that Beethoven confined himself, as a rule, to a single bottle of wine per meal (!) and exceeded this only in company. Add to his health problems the profound emotional wear and tear of the ongoing Karl saga and servant problems and it comes as no surprise that work on the **Missa solemnis**, already long overdue (it was to have been ready for the enthronement of the Archduke Rudolph as Archbishop of Olmütz in 1820), ground almost to a halt. He did, however, complete his Piano Sonata in A flat, Op. 110, in 1821, though he was later to revise the finale. 1822 saw a return to form, with the completion of the *Missa solemnis* and his last **Piano Sonata, Op. 111 in C minor**, as well as the splendid *Consecration of the House* Overture. Also significant was a commission from the Russian Prince Nikolas Galitsin for some new string quartets. In 1823 Beethoven completed the monumental Thirty-Three Variations on a Waltz by Diabelli, Op. 120, and worked in earnest on the **Ninth Symphony**.

It was at around this time that Beethoven received visits from three very different composers: Rossini, Weber, and the eleven-year-old Franz Liszt. Weber was enchanted and rather surprised at the warmth of his reception:

Beethoven welcomed me with the most touching affection; he embraced me at least six or seven times in the heartiest fashion and finally, full of enthusiasm, cried: "Yes, you are a devil of a fellow, a fine fellow!" We spent the noon-hour together, very merrily and happily. This rough, repellent man actually paid court to me, served me at table as carefully as though I were his lady, etc. In short, this day always will remain a most remarkable one for me, as for all who shared in it. It gave me quite a special exaltation to see myself overwhelmed with such affectionate attention by this great spirit.

No less memorable was Beethoven's reception of Liszt. Beethoven, known for his aversion to child prodigies, had refused several times to see Liszt; but Czerny, Liszt's teacher, finally prevailed upon him, and a meeting was arranged. Liszt himself takes up the tale:

It was ten o'clock in the morning when we entered the two small rooms in the Schwarzspanier house which Beethoven occupied, I somewhat shyly, Czerny amiably encouraging me. Beethoven was working at a long, narrow table by the window. He looked gloomily at us for a time, said a few brief words to Czerny and remained silent when my kind teacher beckoned me to the piano. I first played a short piece by Ries. When I had finished, Beethoven asked me whether I could play a Bach fugue. I chose the C minor Fugue from The Well-Tempered Clavier. *"And could you also transpose the Fugue at once into another key?" Beethoven asked me. Fortunately I was able to do so. After my closing chord I glanced up. The great Master's darkly glowering gaze lay piercingly upon me. Yet suddenly a gentle smile passed over his gloomy features. He came quite close to me, stooped down, put his hand on my head, and stroked my hair several times. "A devil of a fellow," he whispered, "a regular young Turk!" Suddenly I felt quite brave. "May I play something of yours now?" I boldly asked. Beethoven smiled and nodded. I played the first movement of the C major Concerto. When I*

had concluded, Beethoven caught hold of me with both hands, kissed me
on the forehead, and said gently: "Go! You are one of the fortunate ones!
For you will give joy and happiness to many other people! There is noth-
ing better or finer!" This event in my life has remained my greatest pride,
the palladium of my whole career as an artist.

On what evidence Beethoven based his prophecy is hard to say.
If he could hear the playing at all, which is doubtful, it can only
have been subject to considerable distortion. Yet much could be
gleaned by a pianist of Beethoven's experience on the basis of
sight alone: not only tempos, but also aspects of
phrasing, articulation, and even volume (the
hands, wrists, and arms of even the most
relaxed pianist playing very loudly will always
look different from the same hands playing
softly). When it came to improvisation,
Beethoven would have had no difficulty in
"hearing" in his mind's ear the rhythms, the harmonies, the
melodies, indeed most if not all of the notes, on the basis of sight
alone, just as an accomplished lip-reader can "hear" not only the
words of a speaker, but their patterns and emphases. Two other
points are worth noting. Beethoven would doubtless have been
charmed and moved by the young Liszt's natural modesty in the
face of his extraordinary achievements. And his remarks, as
quoted by Liszt himself, contain nothing in the way of actual
praise, nor do they comment specifically on his performances.
Even had he hated the playing, it would still have been safe to
predict that Liszt would give happiness and pleasure to many
people, just as Picasso would confidently have been able to say
the same thing to Walter Lantz, the creator of Bugs Bunny, without suggesting that he and Lantz were even in the same ball park.
Such thoughts, however, would not have crossed the mind of an
eleven-year-old boy.

> "Go! You are one of the fortunate ones! For you will give joy and happiness to many other people! There is nothing better or finer!"

Interlude VI:
Chamber Music (2): Strings Alone

Beethoven was not a man easily intimidated. Yet he put off writing a string quartet until he was into his thirties. What stayed his hand were the examples of Haydn, then still alive and active, and Mozart, who between them had brought the new medium to a peak of perfection that only one man stood any chance of equaling. Beethoven had no doubt that he was that man; but he knew, too, that he must be ready. He prepared himself by working almost literally around the string quartet, first with a series of string trios, then with the String Quintet, Op. 4. It was with the publication of the three string trios, Op. 9, in 1798 that he served notice of his arrival as the heir apparent to his two great predecessors. These undeservedly neglected trios are in no way string quartets *manqués* but splendidly full-bodied works in which Beethoven very cleverly manages to make three instruments sound like four.

Beethoven's sequence of sixteen string quartets begins with the set of six, Op. 18, which he published in 1801. That he regarded the medium itself with the utmost seriousness is already evident in the slow movement of No. 1 in F. As in many of his major works, this *Adagio* is the real heart of the whole quartet, which is otherwise genial and sometimes capricious. Beethoven was generally opposed to programmatic music; but he did reveal that in this case he had been inspired by the tomb scene in Shakespeare's *Romeo and Juliet.*

In the Second Quartet, in G, he pays his debts to Mozart and Haydn with the greatest elegance and grace, but introduces characteristically boisterous dramatic touches, particularly towards the end of the first movement and in the comic finale. Perhaps the most adventurous feature of No. 3, in D, is Beethoven's strategic use of unexpected key changes as a structural device. No formal knowledge is necessary to feel the effects of this: the changes of tone, both aural and expressive, come across whether one recognizes their source or not.

This is the Beethoven who would turn up at his patrons' palaces dressed almost like a tramp.

The Fourth Quartet, in Beethoven's favorite key of C minor, is the odd-one-out of the set, introducing for the first time in the sequence a curiously rough-hewn, "uncompromising" tone of voice. This is the Beethoven who would turn up at his patrons' palaces dressed almost like a tramp. At the other end of the spectrum is the graceful, luminous No. 5 in A, Beethoven's homage to his favorite Mozart quartet, K.464, in the same key. The most striking features of the B flat Quartet, Op. 18 No. 6, are, firstly, the rhythmic swing and bounce of the scherzo, whose almost obsessive, jazz-like syncopations seem to say to the listener "count this if you can!"; and secondly, the slow introduction to the dance-like finale, entitled "La malinconia," though the mood of brooding melancholy is so self-evident that the signpost is superfluous. This introduction to a finale is not merely a structural novelty. It is also remarkable for briefly blurring all sense of key, and for its fragmentary recurrence later in the movement. This juxtaposition of extreme contrasts almost has the effect of a debate between the forces of darkness and light.

Five years were to elapse before Beethoven returned to the string quartet, but the distance travelled in terms of content and

conception seems more like light years. The three **"Razumovsky" Quartets** (named after the Russian count who commissioned them) are conceived on a scale without precedent in the medium; and in that expansion of the scale is an expansion of the spiritual, emotional, and psychological range it can encompass. As we have seen, this was in no way an isolated phenomenon. The same holds true for other works that Beethoven composed during this period, including the **"Eroica" Symphony** and the "Waldstein" and **"Appassionata" sonatas**. It would be only a slight exaggeration to say that with each of these works Beethoven transformed the entire concept of what music could do. But whereas the others met with a generally favorable reception from musicians and music lovers alike, the "Razumovsky" Quartets bewildered many musicians who were generally sympathetic to Beethoven's music. Schuppanzigh, Beethoven's favorite quartet leader, apparently thought the First must be some kind of farfetched joke whose point escaped him. Another violinist and quartet player, Felice Radicati, asked Beethoven directly whether he seriously considered these works to be music at all. Beethoven was unfazed: "Oh," he said, "they are not for you, but for a later age!"

He was right. Of the three, only the last, in C major, gained anything like widespread acceptance in his lifetime. An important feature of all three is the degree to which large-scale structures are derived from a small number of relatively short musical "cells." The broad opening tune of No. 1 in F, for instance, forms the basis for much of the movement that follows. Another example is the expansive and often extremely subtle development of the first two chords of No. 2 in E minor. These cellular building blocks need not be melodic or harmonic. The scherzo movement from the same quartet is derived obsessively from the rhythmic figure of its opening bar. But it must be stressed that an ability to spot these organic relationships is no more essential to an appreciation of the music than is a knowledge of facial musculature to an appreciation of the *Mona Lisa*. A further significant aspect of these quartets is the unprecedented technical challenge that they pose to all four players.

The beautiful "Harp" Quartet, Op. 74 of 1809 (so nicknamed because of the arpeggiated *pizzicato* effects in the first movement) is written on the same large scale as its three immediate predecessors, though it ends, uniquely in Beethoven's quartets, with a set of variations. Again the instrumental challenges are considerable, especially for the first violin, who crowns the first movement's coda with a thrilling, concerto-like solo. But the music's expressive world is generally more genial and less probing than that of the "Razumovsky" Quartets.

> Each is the product of arguably the most powerful intellect in musical history, working at full stretch.

The "Serioso" subtitle of the F minor Quartet, Op. 95 of 1810, is as redundant as "La malinconia" is to the finale of Op. 18 No. 6. Its grim seriousness is abundantly clear from the outset, and is unmistakably maintained thereafter. This is Beethoven's most compact and intense quartet, as remarkable for its compression as the "Eroica" Symphony and the "Razumovsky" Quartets are for their revolutionary expansion. Also significant is the amount of cussed humor that finds its way into the music. Revealingly, Beethoven wrote of this quartet that "it was composed for a small circle of connoisseurs and was never intended to be played in public." Indeed, for six years he refused to publish it.

Nearly fifteen years passed before Beethoven returned to the medium, and he then turned out five unique works that for many constitute the greatest music ever written. Each is the product of arguably the most powerful intellect in musical history, working at full stretch; and each opens up hitherto uncharted realms of experience.

The first of the series, the E flat Quartet, Op. 127, is outwardly the simplest, and the most closely related in structure to the middle-period quartets. The serenely lyrical opening movement, preceded by a *Maestoso* introduction that twice recurs later in the movement, is followed by an *Adagio* that is among one of Beethoven's most sublime. The substantial scherzo leads to an irresistibly uplifting finale that combines the elements of both sonata and rondo form. Op. 127 shares the expansiveness of the "Razumovsky" Quartets as well as their polyphonic preoccupations. Like its siblings still to come, it combines what was then extreme modernity—which we can still feel today—with backward glances into ancient roots. The influence of Bach and Handel is occasionally felt; but in these final works Beethoven also reaches back to the pure, vocal counterpoint of Palestrina (born c. 1525) and other masters of the Italian Renaissance. A perfect example is the second movement of Op. 127, a theme and variations of extraordinary beauty.

Between Op. 127 and the last of Beethoven's quartets come three that stand together as a kind of musical trinity. As with the "Razumovskys," it was many years before they found their place anywhere near the centre of the mainstream repertoire. They, still more than the "Razumovskys," were definitely composed "for a later age."

CD 2
track 7
www.naxos.com

The A minor Quartet, Op. 132, the **B flat, Op. 130**, and the C sharp minor, Op. 131, are unconventional not only in the number of their movements (five in Op. 132, six in Op. 130, seven in Op. 131), but also in their form, key scheme and order. The movements' relative durations are also highly irregular. In Op. 132, for instance, the five movements last roughly 9:30, 8:00, 16:00 (the "Heiliger Dankgesang"), 2:00, and around 7:00. In Op. 131 the pattern is still more striking in its diversity: 8:00, 3:00, 0:50, 14:00, 5:00, 2:00, and about 7:00. In both quartets, the longest and most unearthly movements form the structural and spiritual centerpiece.

At this point in Beethoven's musical odyssey, the word "spiritual" is unavoidable. In ways that can never be expressed in verbal language, Beethoven's most exalted music goes *beyond* emotion, though emotion is always a component of it. It seems no exaggeration to say that in these quartets we enter a new dimension of consciousness. The word "awe" does not come amiss here. Nor does "humility." Yet in the case of the great slow movement of Op. 132, Beethoven himself invokes words to enhance the listener's understanding, both of the music itself and of the communicative intention of the composer: "Heiliger Dankgesang eines Genesenden an die Gottheit, in der lydischen Tonart" ("Sacred Song of Thanksgiving by a Convalescent to the Deity, in the Lydian Mode"). As Beethoven well knew, the illness to which he alludes had very nearly been fatal.

> In these quartets we enter a new dimension of consciousness. The word "awe" does not come amiss here.

These three quartets can be seen in some ways as a single gigantic work, a trilogy with thematic links as well as contiguous opus numbers. The chief linking factor is a four-note motif that plays a prominent role in all three, albeit occasionally in disguise. It is introduced by the cello, at the very beginning of Op. 132, and it is at its most dramatic in the gigantic "Grosse Fuge" ("Great Fugue") which originally formed the finale of **Op. 130**. Beethoven was persuaded that this "Grosse Fuge" overbalanced the rest of the quartet, both in its size and its complexity; and with uncharacteristic compliance he agreed to compose a replacement finale, leaving the "Grosse Fuge" to stand on its own as Op. 133. The replacement finale, the last thing Beethoven finished, is delightful music, but is too lightweight to provide the dramatic culmination that he originally envisaged. Many professional string quartets today pres-

CD 2
track 7

www.naxos.com

Finale

On May 7, 1824, **Beethoven's Ninth Symphony** had its long-awaited premiere. It was a strange and in some ways tragic occasion, as the orchestral violinist Josef Böhm recalled:

> *Beethoven himself conducted. That is, he stood in front of a conductor's stand and threw himself back and forth like a madman, flailing about with his hands and feet as though he wanted to play all the instruments and sing all the chorus parts. The actual direction was in the hands of Duport; we musicians followed his baton only. Beethoven was so excited that he saw nothing that was going on around him, paying no heed whatever to the bursts of applause, which his deafness prevented him from hearing in any case. He had always to be told when it was time to acknowledge the applause, which he did in the most ungracious manner imaginable.*

The Ninth Symphony was by some margin the most colossal orchestral work ever written. With its long choral finale, complete with four vocal soloists, it paved the way, as noted earlier, for the massive choral symphonies of Mahler some seven decades later. It was also to be Beethoven's last symphony, though not by design.

In the aftermath of the Ninth Symphony's premiere—the climax of a series of distractions, professional, social, domestic, and financial—Beethoven followed his normal custom and retreated to the country, in this case near the outlying suburb of Baden. Here, spurred by the commission of 1822 from Prince Galitsin, he returned, after a lapse of nearly a decade and a half, to one of the most intimate and exacting forms of music-making: the string quartet. Beethoven's final contributions to that medium, one which he himself had done much to develop, mark the apex of his creative life. They take us into hitherto uncharted realms of spiritual experience, which lie far beyond the powers of analysis to explain or to describe. The violinist Karl Holz, one of the closest friends of his last years, leaves no doubt that Beethoven fully recognized this. "For him," wrote Holz, "the crowning achievement of his quartet writing, and his favorite piece, was the E flat "Cavatina" from the Quartet in B flat major [**Op. 130**]. He actually composed it in tears of melancholy, and confessed to me that his own music had never had such an effect on him before, and that even thinking back to the piece cost him fresh tears."

> They take us into hitherto uncharted realms of spiritual experience, which lie far beyond the powers of analysis to explain or to describe.

To the loss of his hearing, the continual "humming and buzzing" in his ears (of which he first complained in 1800), and his chronic abdominal problems was now added a further torment in the form of ophthalmia, a painful inflammation of the eyes. In 1825 he suffered a severe and potentially fatal illness, from which he was rescued by a strict diet and the total avoidance of alcohol (among other remedies). Writing to his doctor from Baden, where he had been sent to recuperate, he demonstrated, as he had often done, that his sufferings had not deprived him of his sense of humor:

Esteemed Friend!
Baden, May 13, 1825
Doctor: How are you, my patient?

Patient: We are rather poorly—we still feel very weak and are belching and so forth… I spit a good deal of blood, but probably only from my windpipe. I also have frequent nosebleeds… and my stomach has become dreadfully weak, as has, generally speaking, my whole constitution. Judging by what I know, my strength will hardly be restored unaided.

Doctor: I will help you. I will alternate Brown's method with that of Stoll [these being two diametrically opposite forms of treatment].

Patient: I should like to be able to sit at my writing desk again and feel a little stronger. Do bear this in mind.

Finis

He then adds: "The last medicine you prescribed I took only once and then lost." It was characteristic of Beethoven as a patient to seek the advice of his doctors and proceed not to follow it. When he did return to his writing desk, the first thing he wrote was the famous "Heiliger Dankgesang" (see p. 141).

Following the completion of his final quartet, Op. 135, he turned his thoughts once more to the orchestra. At the time of his death he had already made substantial sketches for a tenth symphony, which might well have been completed but for an event that took place some miles from Vienna. On July 30, 1826, in a ruined castle near Baden, Karl, now nineteen, shot himself in the head. Found fully conscious, he was taken to his mother's lodgings nearby. He was a notoriously bad shot, but to shoot oneself in the head and not even lose consciousness suggests not so much a bad aim as a very clear message to his uncle. And the fact that he was delivered into his mother's care rather than into Beethoven's was surely not pure chance. When he was asked by the local magistrate what had led him to this desperate act, his answer was unequivocal: "Because my

His answer was unequivocal: "Because my uncle tormented me too much, and I was weary of imprisonment."

uncle tormented me too much, and I was weary of imprisonment." Beethoven tried to hush up the incident, but he was too
late; and Karl had the satisfaction (if that is indeed how he felt)
of seeing his uncle age practically overnight. From then on,
Beethoven both looked and felt like an old man, and often
described himself as such, though he was only fifty-five when
the incident took place. Shocked he may have been, and guilty
too. But except for minor improvements, his treatment of Karl,
and Johanna, continued much as before. It was, therefore, a
great relief for all concerned (though Beethoven at first was
loth to admit it) when Karl announced his intention to join the
army. There he would be strictly supervised and free at last
from the endless wrangling of his mother and uncle.

In the meantime, while his hair grew long enough to conceal
the signs of his injury, Karl and his uncle journeyed to the town
of Gneixendorf at the invitation of Beethoven's brother Johann
and his wife Therese, with whom his relations had never been
easy. There Beethoven composed his last quartet, Op. 135 in F,
and a new finale for the **B flat Quartet, Op. 130**, to replace the
controversial "Grosse Fuge." The serenity that can be found in
his last music, however, had no significant counterpart in his
personal relationships. Despite the last major attempt at reconciliation, he and his brother quarreled frequently; Therese often
joined the fray, while Karl quarreled with everyone. After a particularly bitter row over Johann's will, Beethoven and Karl
made a hasty departure for Vienna on December 1.

In the words of Andreas Wawruch, Beethoven's last attend-
ing physician:

CD 2
track 7
www.naxos.com

> *December was raw, wet, cold, and frosty. Beethoven's clothing was*
> *anything but suited to the unkind season of the year, and yet he was*
> *driven on and away by an inner restlessness, a sinister presentiment of*
> *misfortune. He was obliged to stop overnight in a village inn, where*

Beethoven's nephew Karl

in addition to the shelter afforded by its wretched roof he found only an unheated room without winter windows. Towards midnight he was seized with convulsive chills and fever, accompanied by violent thirst and pains in the side. When the fever heat began to break, he drank a couple of quarts of ice-cold water, and yearned, in his helpless state, for the first ray of dawn. Weak and ill, he had himself loaded (with Karl's assistance) onto an open milk-wagon, and arrived in Vienna enervated and exhausted.

Once home, Beethoven took to his bed with a severe chill. Three days passed, however, before Karl saw fit to summon medical assistance. Wawruch arrived, and was greatly disturbed:

I found Beethoven with grave symptoms of inflammation of the lungs: his face glowed, he spat blood, when he breathed he threatened to choke, and the shooting pain in his side only allowed him to lie in a tormenting posture flat on his back. A strict anti-inflammatory mode of treatment soon brought the desired improvement; nature was conquered, and a happy crisis freed him of the seemingly imminent danger of death.

On the fifth day he was able to sit up and converse, and on the seventh he was up and about, albeit it minimally, and was once more able to read and write. The improvement was short-lived. When Wawruch arrived the next morning, he was frankly alarmed:

I found him greatly agitated; his entire body was jaundiced, while a terrible fit of vomiting and diarrhea during the preceding night had threatened to kill him. Violent anger, profound suffering because of ingratitude, and an undeserved insult [presumably from Karl] had triggered the tremendous explosion. Shaking and trembling, he now writhed with the pain which raged in his liver and intestines; and his feet, hitherto only moderately puffed up, were now greatly swollen.

From this time on, his dropsy developed; his secretions decreased in quantity, his liver evidenced the presence of hard knots, his jaundice grew worse. His illness now progressed with giant strides. Already, during the third week, nocturnal choking attacks set in; the tremendous volume of the water accumulated called for immediate relief. I found myself compelled to advocate the abdominal puncture in order to preclude the danger of sudden bursting. The liquid amounted to twenty-five pounds in weight, yet the afterflow must have been five times that.

Carelessness in undoing the bandage of the wound at night, probably in order quickly to remove all the water which had gathered, put an end to any optimism regarding Beethoven's condition. A violent erysipelatic inflammation set in and showed incipient signs of gangrene, but the greatest care exercised in keeping the inflamed surfaces dry soon checked the evil. Three succeeding operations were effected without difficulty.

In their last month together before Karl joined the army, Beethoven was mostly confined to bed, and for much of that time Karl was at his side. The old quarrels, suspicions, and reproaches seemed at last to have been laid to rest, though Beethoven's obsession with Johanna's dangerous influence persisted. After Karl went off to join his regiment on January 2, 1827, Beethoven's condition declined sharply. It soon became apparent that he was very gravely ill.

As Schindler wrote to Moscheles in late February: "As is now evident, his dropsy is turning into a wasting away, for now he is no more than skin and bones; yet his constitution bids fair to withstand this terrible end for a very long period of time." In his later years Beethoven grew less gregarious; but particularly after his "wilderness" period of 1812–13, he enjoyed being the focus of attention. Now, as he lay more seriously ill than at any time in his life, his mood was darkened, and his resistance weakened, by what he perceived as a general neglect. As Schindler wrote at the time:

> *What hurts him greatly is the fact that no one here takes any notice of him; and in truth this lack of interest is most striking. Formerly people drove up in their carriages if he were no more than indisposed; now he is totally forgotten, as though he had never lived in Vienna.*

If Beethoven was depressed, however, he was by no means hopeless. He repeatedly spoke of going to England when he was well again (he had received numerous invitations from the musical establishment in London) and was now busy calculating how he might live most cheaply during the trip. For one as inexperienced in foreign travel as he, this was a significant development. He had long known of Haydn's successes in Britain, and saw no reason why he should not enjoy the same. In the meantime, he distracted himself, when alone, in reading–mostly the ancient Greeks (a lifelong enthusiasm) and the novels of Sir Walter Scott, which he greatly enjoyed.

Now, as he lay more seriously ill than at any time in his life, his mood was darkened.

On March 8, 1827, the young pianist Ferdinand von Hiller, then only fifteen but later a major artist, was taken by his teacher Hummel to meet the master. Warned ahead of time that Beethoven's appearance was such as to evoke near-horror in his visitors, Hiller was relieved to find the reality less shocking:

> *Through a commodious ante-room in which tall closets held thick, corded masses of music, we came (how my heart beat!) into*

Beethoven's living room, and were not a little surprised to see the Master to all appearances quite comfortably seated at the window. He wore a long, grey dressing-gown, completely open at the moment, and high boots which reached to his knees. Emaciated by his dreadful malady, he seemed to me, as he rose, to be tall in stature. He was unshaven, his heavy, partly grey hair hung in disorder over his temples; but the expression of his features when he caught sight of Hummel grew very mild and gentle, and he seemed extraordinarily glad to see him. The two men embraced with the utmost heartiness; Hummel presented me; Beethoven was entirely gracious and I was allowed to sit down opposite him at the window.

Of the embittered and paranoid, half-mad man, there was no sign. Beethoven showed genuine interest in his young guest and treated him with great respect and dignity.

On March 13, Hummel took Hiller to Beethoven again. The boy was shocked by the change. "The Master lay in bed, evidently suffering violent pain and occasionally giving a deep groan, although he talked a good deal, and with animation." Among other things, he lamented his lack of a wife, and expressed his great envy of Hummel, whose wife he admired. Since their last visit to him, Beethoven had been given a picture of the modest village house in which Haydn had been born. It now hung on the wall beside his bed. In these dark days it had become one of his prize possessions. "I was as pleased as any child," he said. "To think that so great a man could come from such humble beginnings!" Any resentments of his former teacher had by now been long forgotten. The greatest gift of his final months, however, had been sent to him from London by the harp-maker Johann Stumpff: Samuel Arnold's complete edition of the works of Handel, in forty volumes. This set the seal on his conviction that Handel was the greatest of all composers. He wrote to thank Stumpff:

February 8, 1827, Vienna

My very dear Friend!

My pen is quite unable to describe the great pleasure afforded me by the volumes of Handel's works which you have sent me as a gift—to me a royal gift!... Unfortunately since December 3 I have been confined to bed with dropsy. You can imagine the situation to which this illness has reduced me. Usually I live entirely on the profits of my intellectual work. But unfortunately, for the last two and a half months I have not been able to write a single note. My income only suffices to pay my half-yearly rent, leaving me a few hundred gulden. Bear in mind too that the end of my illness is not by any means in sight. Nor do I know when it will be possible for me again to soar through the air on Pegasus in full flight! Physician, surgeon, everything has to be paid for.

I well remember that several years ago the Philharmonic Society wanted to give a concert for my benefit. It would be fortunate for me if they would now decide to do so. Perhaps I might still be rescued from the poverty with which I am now faced. I am writing to Mr Smart about this. And if you, dear friend, can contribute something to this object, do please come to an agreement with Mr S. A letter about this is being written to Moscheles as well. And if all my friends combine, I do believe that it will be possible to do something for me in this matter.

The Philharmonic Society, on learning of his condition, immediately dispatched to him the then very considerable sum of £100 as a gift. In his last dated letter, Beethoven wrote to Moscheles:

Vienna, March 18, 1827

My dear, kind Moscheles!

I cannot put into words the emotion with which I read your letter of March 1. The Philharmonic Society's generosity in almost anticipating my appeal has touched my innermost soul. I request you, therefore, dear Moscheles, to be the spokesman through whom I send to the Philharmonic Society my warmest and most heartfelt thanks for their particular sympathy and support....May Heaven but restore my health very soon and I shall prove to those magnanimous Englishmen how greatly I appreciate their sympathy for me in my sad fate. But your noble behavior I shall never forget; and I will shortly proceed to express my thanks particularly to Sir Smart [sic] and Herr Stumpff.

I wish you all happiness! With the most friendly sentiments I remain your friend who highly esteems you

LUDWIG VAN BEETHOVEN

In addition to the natural torments he suffered from his illness, Beethoven endured four abdominal operations that brought him no more than temporary relief. As March drew to a close, his friends, among them Anton Schindler, could hardly doubt that Beethoven too was near his end:

His death was rapidly approaching, and we could only wish to see him released from his terrible suffering. For a week he lay as though almost dead, but would summon his remaining strength now and again to put a question or to ask for something. His condition was quite terrible. He lay in a permanent state of dull brooding; his head hanging forward onto his breast and his eyes staring fixedly at one spot for hours; he seldom recognized his closest acquaintances unless he was told who they were. It was a dreadful thing to see.

On March 23, in a particularly lucid moment, he asked for his pen and painfully wrote his final words—a codicil to his will, in which he specified that in the event of Karl's death the entire capital of his estate should pass to his sister-in-law Johanna van

Beethoven. At long last, he had made his peace with "the Queen of the Night." The moment had now come when Beethoven, the man who had taken Fate by the throat, knew with absolute certainty that his lifelong struggle was almost over. He turned to the friends standing at his bedside, and surprised them by speaking in Latin: "Plaudite amici, finita est comoedia" ("Applaud, my friends, for the comedy is over"). Soon afterwards he lost consciousness and lapsed into a coma. Yet still he clung to life. Two days passed. The morning of the 26th dawned stormy, and the unsettled, wintry weather persisted through the day. The rest of the story can be told by the composer Anselm Hüttenbrenner, a close friend of Schubert's:

> *During Beethoven's last moments there was no one present in the death-chamber but Frau van Beethoven and myself. Beethoven lay in the final agony, unconscious and with the death-rattle in his throat, from three o'clock, when I arrived, until after 5 o'clock. Then there was suddenly a loud clap of thunder accompanied by a bolt of lightning which illuminated the death-chamber with a harsh light (the snow lay thick in front of Beethoven's house). After this unexpected natural phenomenon, which had shaken me greatly, Beethoven suddenly opened his eyes, raised his right hand, looked upwards for several seconds and shook his fist, with a very grave, threatening countenance, as though to say "I defy you all, powers of evil! Away! God is with me." And his hand sank down onto the bed again, his eyes half closed. My right hand lay under his head, my left rested on his breast. There was no more breathing, no more heartbeat. The great composer's spirit fled from this world of deception into the kingdom of truth. I shut his half-open eyes, kissed them, and then his forehead, mouth, and hands. At my request, Frau van Beethoven cut a lock of his hair and gave it to me as a sacred relic of Beethoven's last hour.*

Over three decades earlier, the streets of Vienna had been almost deserted when the body of the thirty-five-year-old Mozart was conveyed in the rain to an unmarked grave. Now, on March 29, 1827, they were choked by an estimated 20,000 mourners who gathered to pay their last respects to the man almost universally regarded as the greatest composer of his time. He was a man, as we have seen, whose life had been beset by almost continuous sufferings–physical, psychological, and emotional–but a man, also, whose ultimately indomitable love of life had found unique expression in his music. His art embraced the whole of life, and the experience of all humanity; and it is no coincidence that the last movement of his **last symphony** is a setting of Schiller's *Ode to Joy*. Its principal melody, now adopted as the European anthem, remains the most famous that he ever wrote.

Friedrich von Schiller (1759–1805), poet who wrote Ode to Joy

Epilogue:
The Truly Immortal Beloved

If Beethoven had lived to the same age as Haydn and retained all his mental faculties, he could have known the maturest works of Chopin, the complete works of Mendelssohn, most of the piano, chamber, and orchestral works of Schumann (as well as most of the songs), Wagner's *Flying Dutchman* and *Tannhäuser*, the symphonies and most of the choral works of Berlioz, even Verdi's *Nabucco* and *Macbeth*. Had he lived to the same age as Sibelius he could have taken in numerous pieces by Brahms (including the D minor Piano Concerto and the "Handel" Variations), Liszt's Sonata in B minor, both of his concertos and symphonies, and Verdi's *Rigoletto, Il trovatore,* and *La traviata.* With the exception of Verdi, he was a formative influence on all of them. And composers as recent as Sir Michael Tippett (1905–1998) and Robert Simpson (1921–1997) have claimed him as the principal shaping force on their own development.

Because he died at fifty-six, unlike the tragically young Schubert (dead at thirty-one) and Mozart (thirty-five), one rarely encounters any serious speculation as to how Beethoven might have developed if he *had* lived as long as Haydn. His influence on posterity has already been immense. None of the composers just mentioned would have written quite as they did had he not existed. Would they, however, have written as they did if he had gone on composing for another quarter-century, as their contemporary? To say the least, there is no evidence that he was running out of steam. What if his already unprecedented odyssey had led him to atonality before Liszt, let alone Schoenberg? It would significantly have changed the course of twentieth-century music. As it is, he basically set the agenda for the nineteenth. In Liszt's words, "For us musicians, Beethoven's work is like the pillar of cloud and fire which guided the Israelites through the desert... His darkness and his light trace for us equally the path we have to follow." And from Wagner, after first hearing the **Seventh Symphony** in 1828:

> "For us musicians, Beethoven's work is like the pillar of cloud and fire which guided the Israelites through the desert... His darkness and his light trace for us equally the path we have to follow."

CD 2
track 4
www.naxos.com

The effect on me was indescribable. To this must be added the impression produced on me by Beethoven's features, which I saw in the lithographs that were circulated everywhere at that time... I soon conceived an image of him in my mind as a sublime and unique supernatural being.

"Sublime" and "supernatural"–the sacred twins of the Romantic era. It was perhaps Wagner more than anyone else, in his writings and his conducting, who shaped the nineteenth-century image of Beethoven. Close behind him was his father-in-law Liszt, whose career as both performer and composer was fueled by his proselytizing zeal for Beethoven's music. Nor should we overlook the contribution of Berlioz, another crusading conductor of genius. Like Wagner (and to a lesser extent like Liszt), Berlioz was not only a composer and conductor but a prolific and often fantastical writer. Typical was his characterization of the String Quartet, Op. 131 as "a heavenly inspiration that took material shape." This almost ritualistic combining of the sublime and the supernatural served both to emphasize the spirituality of Beethoven's music and to bathe the image of its creator in an implicitly religious light. In this perspective, Beethoven is cast neither as saint (which in life he was manifestly not) nor hero (which in his struggle with adversity he was) but as a truly Godlike figure (which is how he sometimes saw himself). Though styling himself as a "Bacchus," he consciously modeled himself, as he confessed in 1818, on Socrates and Jesus Christ, no less. He, in turn, became a model for such bastions of French Romantic literature as Alfred de Vigny, Alphonse de Lamartine, and Victor Hugo.

> "Beethoven's Second Symphony is a crass monster, a hideously writhing wounded dragon, that refuses to expire."

Unlike Bach, Schubert, Mahler, and Bruckner, Beethoven's importance as a composer was widely acknowledged in his lifetime and all but universally acknowledged after his death. His influence was incalculable. But an influential composer is not by that token a beloved one. No one could seriously dispute the influence and consequent importance of Arnold Schoenberg, but his prophecy, "Someday milkmaids will hum my tunes," has proved wide of the mark—and not just because milkmaids have gone out of fashion. His music, almost a century after his first revolutionary experiments with atonality, is loved by a minuscule percentage of the musical public. Beethoven, as we have seen, had his problems with the public too. One can understand this in the case of the late works. The "Grosse Fuge" is still a hard nut to crack. One can understand it, too, with the **"Eroica"** and the **"Razumovsky" Quartets.** But with the **Second Symphony**, one of the happiest and most exuberant pieces in the repertoire? According to the critic of the *Zeitung für die elegante Welt* in Vienna, writing in May 1804, "Beethoven's Second Symphony is a crass monster, a hideously writhing wounded dragon, that refuses to expire, and though bleeding in the Finale, furiously beats about with its tail erect."

CD 1
track 5
www.naxos.com

CD 1
track 9
www.naxos.com

CD 1
track 7
www.naxos.com

We have already encountered August von Kotzebue in another Viennese journal, claiming strength in numbers and arraigning by implication all of Beethoven's works: "Impartial musicians and music lovers are all agreed that there was never anything so incoherent, shrill, chaotic, and earsplitting as Beethoven's music." It was not for his musical views, however, but as a spy that Kotzebue's life was ended by an assassin's bullet in 1819. Time was hardly a great healer in the case of Beethoven's posthumous critics. Three decades after Beethoven's death, the esteemed composer Louis Spohr wrote:

> *I freely confess that I could never get any enjoyment out of Beethoven's last works. And I include among them even the much-admired Ninth Symphony, the fourth movement of which seems to me so ugly, in such bad taste, and so cheap, in the conception of Schiller's* Ode, *that I cannot understand even now how such a genius as Beethoven could write it down. It only confirms what I had noticed in Vienna: that Beethoven was deficient in aesthetic imagery and lacked a sense of beauty.*

Spohr's feelings about the **Ninth Symphony** are shared by a significant minority of music lovers even today. His final claim is beyond belief. It is not, however, unique. Still later, in 1913, the American musician and writer James Huneker asserted:

> *Beethoven's music is not beautiful. He is dramatic, powerful, a maker of storms, a subduer of tempests; but his speech is the speech of a self-centered egotist. He is the father of all the megalomaniacs, who looking into their own souls, write what they see therein—misery, corruption, slighting, selfishness, and ugliness.*

It was not only the sound of Beethoven's music but its appearance on the page that troubled some of his detractors. One such held forth in a British periodical *The Harmonicon* in 1823, on the subject of the last **Piano Sonata, Op. 111**:

The second movement is an Arietta, and extends to the extraordinary length of thirteen pages. The greater portion of it is written in 9/16, but a part is in 6/16, and about a page in 12/32. All this really is laborious trifling, and ought to be by every means discouraged by the sensible part of the musical profession. We have devoted a full hour to this enigma, and cannot solve it. But no sphinx ever imagined such a riddle as the 12/32 time presents. Here we find twelve demisemiquavers [sixteenth-notes], and eight double-demisemiquavers [thirty-second-notes] in one bar; twelve demisemiquavers and twelve double-demisemiquavers in another, etc., and all without any appearance of a misprint! The general practice of writing notes apparently very short, then doubling their length by the word Adagio, *is one of the abuses in music that loudly cries for reform; but the system of notation pursued in this Arietta is confusion worse confounded; and yet the publishers have, in their title, deemed it necessary to warn off all pirates by announcing the Sonata as copyright. We do not think they are in much danger of having their property invaded.*

Wilhelm von Lenz was similarly bothered in 1855:

When one is Beethoven, it is possible to do anything, but still two and two must make four. Put two scorpions and a pigeon in the signature if this is your whim, but do not put there what is not in the measure.... You who understand this, explain to us, how can there be, in the second variation in 6/16, six sixteenth-notes in each measure plus six thirty-second notes? The madness of a genius is of interest; but the spectacle of madness in others, which is unfortunately frequent in piano music, is merely deplorable.

Not only was Beethoven condemned for the music he wrote, and the way he wrote it down, he was blamed for its effect on the music of others. As observed in a letter to the London *Quarterly Musical Magazine and Review* within months of Beethoven's death:

> *It is not surprising that Beethoven should have entertained blasé notions of his art; that he should have mistaken noise for grandeur, extravagance for originality, and have supposed that the interest of his compositions would be in proportion to their duration. That he gave little time to reflection, is proved most clearly by the extraordinary length of some movements in his later symphonies... His great qualities are frequently alloyed by a morbid desire for novelty; by extravagance, and by a disdain of rule....The effect which the writings of Beethoven have had on the art must, I fear, be considered as injurious. Led away by the force of his genius and dazzled by its creations, a crowd of imitators has arisen, who have displayed as much harshness, as much extravagance, and as much obscurity, with little or none of his beauty and grandeur. Thus music is no longer intended to soothe, to delight, to "wrap the senses in Elysium"; it is absorbed in one principle—to astonish.*

"The effect which the writings of Beethoven have had on the art must, I fear, be considered as injurious."

Nothing in this letter is more astonishing in its own right than the assertion that Beethoven "gave little time to reflection." As his sketchbooks make clear, he may possibly have given more time to reflection than any great composer before or since. No one, including Schoenberg, was more attentive to the demands of form and musical logic while striving to express with unprecedented intensity every shade of human experience.

Beethoven's works were slow to make much headway in France. As in Vienna, he found early favor amongst the young; but met with opposition from the conservative musical establishment, with Cherubini, director of the Paris Conservatoire from 1822, at their head. The irony would not have been lost on Beethoven, who regarded Cherubini as the greatest of his contemporaries, and valued his Requiem above Mozart's.

What turned the tide was a series of concerts inaugurated in 1828, in which the violinist-conductor François-Antoine Habeneck presented in Paris the first fully professional and thoroughly rehearsed performances of Beethoven's symphonies ever given in France. Even Wagner, who was no Francophile, pronounced them the best he had ever heard. Habeneck did not confine himself to the symphonies. He mounted performances of the hitherto neglected Violin Concerto, the oratorio *Christ on the Mount of Olives*, the Third Piano Concerto, excerpts from the two masses, the "canon" quartet from **Fidelio**, the *Egmont* and *Coriolan* Overtures, and other works. In the audience was Hector Berlioz, who became the most impassioned proponent of Beethoven in France. However, the French conversion was not confined to musicians: painters and writers too were in raptures. After hearing the **Fifth Symphony**, Balzac declared: "Beethoven is the only man who has ever made me feel jealous.…There is in this man a divine force!…What we writers depict is finite, determined; what Beethoven gives us is infinite."

There remained, of course, pockets of resistance for many years after Beethoven's death. Occupying one was the violinist, composer and critic Henri-Louis Blanchard, who sounded off in 1849:

> *Beethoven extends his Quartet No. 13 [Op. 130] to six movements. The first of these movements is remarkable for its search of strange harmonies, for the tiresome delay in the resolution of chords, for a sort of systematic hatred of ending a fragment of a melodic phrase by a perfect cadence, all of which is evidence of worn-out creative ability no longer capable of finding melodies. The fifth and the sixth movements in particular abound in these curious delays in concluding a phrase. To quote an ingeniously picturesque saying of one of our foremost composers whose fine instrumental music is admired by everyone, Beethoven's imagination in the finale of this quartet suggests a poor swallow flitting incessantly in a hermetically sealed compartment to the annoyance of our eyes and our ears.*

CD 1
track 8
www.naxos.com

CD 2
track 2
www.naxos.com

By midcentury, Blanchard and his ilk were in an ever-shrinking minority, not only in France but throughout Europe and across the Atlantic.

In Beethoven, the Romantic concept of the artist as hero found its most potent embodiment. Even as he lived, paintings, drawings, and engravings of him abounded. In their combined variety and similarity they leave little doubt as to his appearance (uniquely, Joseph Dannhauser's lithograph of Beethoven on his deathbed even lets us glimpse his teeth). With both life and death masks to use as models (the former made in 1812, see p. 94), it was easy enough for later artists to achieve a remarkably faithful likeness without ever having set eyes on him. Posthumous busts, heads, statues, engravings, monuments, plaques, postage stamps—all pay tribute to the mythological status that Beethoven enjoyed throughout most of the nineteenth century. Some place him in a classical/allegorical setting (not inappropriately, given his passion for Plato, Homer, and Plutarch); one depicts him stripped to the waist and sitting on a throne, with angels' heads at its back. Perhaps the most famous of Beethoven monuments is Ernst Hähnel's statue, unveiled in Bonn on August 12, 1845. Here the master is depicted fully clothed, indeed heavily cloaked, and mounted on a pedestal surrounded by classical figures of women playing musical instruments. Curiously, Vienna lagged well behind other musical centers in honoring one of its greatest immigrants. Not until 1880, more than half a century after Beethoven's death, did it unveil its own tribute. But what it had lacked in speed it made up for in extravagance: a gargantuan bronze figure seated atop a granite pedestal more than twenty feet in height and attended by twelve smaller figures and an assortment of angels and cherubim. The belatedness of the tribute would not have surprised Beethoven in the slightest.

His influence was not confined merely to music and the visual arts. First in Germany, later in France, still later in Russia, he became the subject of poems, plays, short stories, novels—and, of course, biographies. Unfortunately, the most famous and influential of these for many decades—Anton Schindler's *Life of Beethoven* (first published in 1840)—is largely a work of fiction. The list of Schindler's falsifications is dismaying, not least because it includes many of the stories, pronouncements, and supposed conversations that became standard issue in Beethoven biographies for the next 150 years. Many have long since entered Beethovenian folklore, where they are likely to flourish for decades to come.

The godly associations already noted in the realm of the visual arts persist in much of the literature—particularly, perhaps, in France, following the leads of Vigny, Lamartine, Hugo, and, to a lesser extent, Balzac. The French connection, where Beethoven is concerned, culminated in the work of Romain Rolland. His biography *Beethoven the Creator* (1904) was followed by a ten-volume novel, *Jean-Christophe*, which in many respects was clearly based on Beethoven, and won Rolland the Nobel Prize for Literature in 1912.

Beethoven's power to inspire is a matter of historical record. But to inspire what? In China, in the 1970s, his music was condemned for its representation (among other things) of "the decadent, chaotic life and depraved sentiments of the bourgeoisie." Most western composers were vilified, but none as stridently as Beethoven. For none was more feared. No other had his power to excite, to uplift, to nourish the soul and embolden the spirit. No other so transcendently represented the triumph of the individual over seemingly insuperable odds. He did not need the explicitness of *Fidelio* to make the point (though no opera makes it so stirringly). Nor did he require words. In work after work, his indomitable spirit lends courage to others. No other composer has matched the universality of his appeal, across the globe. His music is for all, and forever. So be it.

The Eighteenth-Century Background

Overview

The eighteenth century has rightly been called "the century of revolutions" (though the nineteenth can lay equal claim to the title), but the most lasting of these were agricultural, industrial, and scientific, not military or political. Human knowledge expanded to an unprecedented degree, with effects on daily life that would eventually eclipse the transient decisions of governments and rulers. Wars, as ever, proliferated, with five in particular having the most lasting impact: the Wars of the Spanish and Austrian Succession, the Seven Years War, and the American and French Revolutions. Despite the gathering groundswell of democracy, absolute monarchies continued to flourish in most parts of the world. Prussia and Russia (the latter, ironically, under the Prussian-born Catherine the Great) became world powers; French power diminished under the increasingly inept rule of Louis XV and Louis XVI; the British Empire expanded, most dramatically in India; and America became a major player on the international political stage. More important, however, than any armed insurrection or expansionist military campaign was the emergence of an increasingly powerful and independent middle class. More than any previous century, the eighteenth was a century of commerce.

World trade was an immediate beneficiary of the improvements in transport and communications that flowed from the scientific and technological advances then taking place on almost every front. By mid-century, raw materials were being imported from countries all over the world, often to the social and economic disadvantage of the exporting nations. Europe, on the other hand, profited hugely, exporting a wide range of goods and spawning a large quantity of financial institutions— banks, stock exchanges, insurance companies, and so on. Checks were increasingly used in place of cash, and the proliferation of paper money increased the amounts that a pedestrian could easily carry. For the newly well-to-do, shopping became a pastime as well as a business.

Among many significant medical advances that substantially improved the quality of life, the most important was the discovery of a vaccine against smallpox—but not before one epidemic in 1719 killed 14,000 people in Paris alone. An unforeseen side effect of middle-class affluence and improved standards of public and personal hygiene was an increase in population that threatened to outstrip the food supply. Although many did indeed starve, the era saw greater changes in agricultural methods than had occurred for many centuries. Farming became a major industry as the demand for food and wool increased.

Of all eighteenth-century revolutions, though, none had more far-reaching consequences than the Industrial Revolution. Originating in Britain in the middle third of the century, it owed its initial impetus to the invention of the steam engine, first used as a means of draining mines but rapidly put to use in factories. With the unprecedented proliferation of new machinery that vastly increased the speed and output of manufacturing, England became known as "the workshop of the world," and prospered accordingly. The revolution soon spread to other countries, shifting the balance of power from the aristocratic landowner to the industrial capitalist and creating a large urban (and increasingly vocal) working class.

Yet despite a burgeoning, increasingly prosperous middle class, which made much of "good manners" and the trappings of gentility, the great majority of the population, in Europe as elsewhere, continued to live in poverty and die early from disease and starvation. Education for the poor was minimal, illiteracy and crime were rife, child labor commonplace, and political representation generally nonexistent. In the Old World and the New, slavery continued unchecked, although an increasing number of Europeans, particularly in Britain, found the practice repugnant.

In Europe and other parts of the world, the traditional ruling classes came increasingly under threat. Of the numerous insurrections that erupted in the eighteenth century, the first of world significance was the American Revolution (1776–83). From it emerged the newly independent United States, a country of vast resources, whose political creed, resoundingly based on libertarian principles and clearly set out in its Declaration of Independence and formal Constitution, served as a beacon to oppressed minorities elsewhere. The American Revolution undoubtedly emboldened the disaffected in France, whose own revolution, initiated by the storming of the Bastille in July 1789 and lasting effectively until Napoleon's seizure of power ten years later, was to be the bloodiest in history. In 1793 alone, during the infamous Reign of Terror, more than 18,000 people were publicly beheaded. In the meantime, the revolutionary government (in reality a sequence of governments) was simultaneously at war with most of Europe, which justifiably feared that the revolution might spread beyond French borders.

Science and Technology

The eighteenth century was a veritable festival of exploration and discovery, in medicine, mechanics, physics, chemistry, and many other fields, including weaponry. Here, as elsewhere, ingenuity sometimes outstripped practicality, as in the ill-fated, one-man, hand-cranked Turtle submarine launched into the depths off the east coast of America in 1755. More useful was Harrison's marine chronometer of 1735, which enabled sailors to pinpoint their exact position at sea; more lethal were Wilkinson's precision-boring cannon of 1774 and Bushnell's invention of the torpedo in 1777. On more peaceable fronts, the period saw the discovery and first use of electricity, most famously by Benjamin Franklin, inventor of the lightning conductor, and the Italian Alessandro Volta, who invented the electrical battery and whose surname, minus the "a," has long since become a household word. Another similarly honored was James Watt, whose improvement of Newcomen's steam engine in 1764 precipitated the Industrial Revolution (the term "watt," incidentally, refers to a unit of power rather than to anything exclusively electrical). Other notable inventions include Claude Chappe's telegraph (a mechanical form of semaphore used to relay coded messages over long distances) and the hydraulic press.

Religion

Religion, as ever, remained both inspirational and contentious. Though there were signs of increased tolerance in certain quarters—as in England, which saw the founding of Methodism by John Wesley in the 1730s and of the Shaker sect in 1772, and, rather surprisingly, in Russia, where Catherine the Great granted freedom of worship in 1766—religious bigotry continued to flourish, particularly in the relations of Protestants and Roman Catholics. The year 1731 saw the expulsion of 20,000 Protestants from Salzburg (most of whom emigrated to America), while the Jacobite rising in the mid-1740s, like the viciously anti-Catholic Gordon Riots of 1780, demonstrated the limits of religious tolerance in Britain. Nor was the appeal in 1781 by the German philosopher Moses Mendelssohn (grandfather of the composer Felix) for better treatment of the Jews either the first or the last. While not as widespread as in the previous century, superstition was still rife amongst the less-educated classes throughout the western world.

Ideas

The eighteenth century, following on from the rationalist trends of the seventeenth, was the age of the Enlightenment, one of the richest eras in the history of western philosophy. Thinkers in every sphere of endeavor, influenced by the quickening flood of scientific discovery, placed ever greater faith in reason as the gateway to truth and natural justice. Highly critical of the *status quo* and hostile to religion, which they saw as enslaving humanity with the chains of superstition, their writings reached a wide audience and contributed directly to the underlying ideals of the American and French Revolutions. Though based mainly in France, where its principal proponents were Diderot, Voltaire, and Rousseau, the movement attracted other important thinkers, most notably the Scots David Hume and Adam Smith, the American Thomas Paine, and the Germans Immanuel Kant and Gotthold Lessing. Voltaire and Rousseau, in particular, used satire as a potent political weapon, and Diderot presided over one of the greatest works of scholarship ever produced: the twenty-eight-volume *Encyclopédie*, inspired by the English encyclopedia published by Ephraim Chambers in 1728 and including seventeen volumes of text and eleven of illustration. Rousseau's *Discourses on the Origins of Inequality* (1754) pilloried the decadent effects of civilization and proclaimed the superiority of the "noble savage." His *Social Contract* of 1762 emphasized the rights of people over government and exhorted people everywhere to overthrow all governments not representing the genuine will of the population. Both books are among the most influential ever written. Adam Smith was an economist whose great work *The Wealth of Nations* (1776) took the revolutionary step of defining wealth in terms of labor, and advocating individual enterprise and free trade as essentials of a just society. Hume's best-known philosophical work, *A Treatise of Human Nature* (1740), is an attack on traditional metaphysics and suggests that all true knowledge resides in personal experience. Kant, on the other hand, argued that right action cannot be based on feelings, inclinations or mere experience but only on a law given by reason, the so-called "categorical imperative." The subject of Thomas Paine's famous book *The Rights of Man* is self-explanatory.

The Arts

The eighteenth century saw the birth and early development of the modern novel with the works of Daniel Defoe (*Robinson Crusoe, Moll Flanders*) and Samuel Richardson (*Pamela, Clarissa*). Above all, however, it was a century of great poets. From the 1770s Goethe, Schiller, and other German poets sowed the seeds of the Romantic movement that was to find its musical manifestation in the nineteenth century. They were followed chronologically by the Britons Blake, Wordsworth, and Coleridge. But it was also the century of the great philosopher-satirists, of whom the greatest were Voltaire (*Candide*), Swift

(*Gulliver's Travels*), and Rousseau (see above). Satire was also conspicuous in the realm of painting, as in the work of William Hogarth (*The Rake's Progress*). The greater painters and sculptors were among the finest portraitists who ever lived: David, Gainsborough, Reynolds, Chardin (who prophetically turned his attentions away from the upper classes and painted the lower bourgeoisie and working classes), Goya (whose grimly apocalyptic visions came in the next century), and Houdon, whose sculptures of Voltaire, Jefferson, and Washington seem almost eerily lifelike. Amongst the century's greatest scholars and men of letters was Samuel Johnson, whose monumental *Dictionary of the English Language* (1755) was the first ever compiled. In the realm of dance, the eighteenth century saw the rise of modern ballet, centered, like so much else, in France. The most influential figures were the ballerina Marie-Anne Camargo (who in 1720 took the revolutionary step of shortening the traditional flowing, court-style dresses to reveal the feet and legs), the choreographer Jean-Georges Noverre (Mozart provided music for his *Les Petits Riens*), and the composer Jean-Philippe Rameau.

Architecture

Except in the upper reaches of society, domestic architecture in eighteenth-century Europe changed relatively little. Public buildings and the dwellings of the well-to-do changed dramatically, on both sides of the Atlantic. The grandiose and ornate gestures of the Baroque era gave way to simpler styles, many of them strongly influenced by the graceful majesty of Classical Greek and Roman designs. Famous examples are the White House and Capitol building of Washington D.C., "Monticello," Thomas Jefferson's home in Virginia (designed by himself), and the Royal Crescent at Bath in England. With the proliferation of new cities spawned by the Industrial Revolution, and the steady expansion of the United States, architects and town planners turned their attentions to the design of not only buildings but towns and cities themselves. The gridiron pattern of Manhattan Island in New York is the fruit of just such planning, and was to be duplicated in many American cities. Here the regularity and symmetry of the neo-Classical approach had a thoroughly practical purpose: with this scheme, cities could be indefinitely extended in any direction. A striking feature of industrial architecture, in particular, was the use of new materials such as cast-iron.

Music

The eighteenth century saw the culmination of the Baroque in the great works of Bach and Handel, and the finest flowering of the Classical era that succeeded it. Domenico Scarlatti was the exact contemporary of Bach and Handel; but such was the astounding originality and exotic nature of the keyboard sonatas that have kept his name alive that he stands largely out-side mainstream trends and developments. In some respects, his most important music is closer in spirit and style to the nineteenth-century Romantics than to anything else written in his own time. If the defining feature of the Baroque style (or, to be more accurate, the Baroque family of styles) was a combi-nation of grandiosity and counterpoint (see Glossary) with a high degree of ornamentation, the Classical style represents an era whose relative simplicity of harmony, texture, and style was entirely in keeping with the ascent of the middle class and the progressive weakening of the aristocracy. The learned, long-lined contrapuntal weaves of the Baroque gave way to the more straightforward texture of melody and accompaniment, the lat-ter often simple broken chords in a pattern known as the

Alberti bass (see Glossary); and the basic harmonic vocabulary became much simplified. Most music written in the Classical era (roughly 1750–1820) is based on an economical framework of four or five basic chords (triads; see Glossary) and draws its material from two or three relatively short, self-contained melodic "themes," frequently of a simple, folk-like character. Not only themes but phrases tend to become shorter and more regular than in most Baroque music. Large-scale structures, too, become generally clearer and more symmetrical, showing analogies with the Classical architecture of the ancient Greeks and Romans. Along with a somewhat ritualized approach to form comes a more formal, more "objective" approach to the expression of emotion. It is often easier to describe the contour of a Classical theme than it is to associate it with a particular mood. The prevailing virtues are symmetry, order, refinement, and grace. The most significant contribution of the Classical era to the history of music is the crystallization of sonata form (see Glossary), brought to its highest peak by Mozart, Haydn, and Beethoven. Virtually all the great works of the Classical era are based on it. The principal genres of the period—sonata, string quartet, concerto, and symphony—are all, in fact, sonatas, differing only in the size and character of the chosen instrumental medium. Standing largely apart from this development is the parallel evolution of opera, dominated in the first half of the century by Handel and Rameau and in the latter by Mozart and Gluck (1714–1787). Because he confined himself for the most part to opera, Gluck's name tends to get left out when people refer loosely to the Classical era, but he was one of the giants. His greatness lies in the quality of his music, but his long-term significance derives from his radical reforms. These did much to simplify and purify an art that had become overladen with irrelevant conventions, complicated by labyrinthine love plots, and disfigured by an excessive attention to virtuosity for its own sake. He derived his plots from classical Greek mythology (*Orfeo ed Euridice, Iphigénie en Aulide, Armide,* etc.), fashioned the music to the emotional and dramatic requirements of his libretto, softened the distinction between recitative and aria (see Glossary), paid scrupulous attention to subtleties of character development, and elevated the role of the chorus (another nod to the classical Greeks). Mozart, despite producing operas that many consider to be the greatest ever written, was not fundamentally a reformer.

The Nineteenth-Century Foreground

Overview

The nineteenth century, especially in Europe and North America, was an era of unprecedented change, peppered, inevitably, with wars and revolutions of almost every kind and at every level of society. The continuing advance of the Industrial Revolution, while far from abolishing poverty, brought new wealth to an ever-expanding middle class. Factories proliferated throughout Europe, soon exceeding the supply of indigenous raw materials and thereby intensifying the impulse towards colonization. The British Empire increased its dominions dramatically, Africa was carved up by Britain and other European colonists, and, despite increasing unease, the slave trade continued. Alarmed by European expansionism, China and Japan attempted to shut out the West altogether. But empire-building went on apace within Europe itself, never more dramatically than during the Napoleonic Wars (1799–1815), which had the incidental effect of igniting in countries from Italy to Russia a fervent nationalism that was to become a running feature of the century as a whole.

Science and Technology

Science and technology, as in the previous century, expanded human knowledge to an unprecedented degree. When Joseph

Lalande published his catalogue of 47,390 stars in 1801, he heralded a century of astronomical discovery both literal and figurative.

Agriculture, easily sidelined by the achievements of the Industrial Revolution, experienced revolutions of its own, with breeding experiments leading to ever bigger crops and fatter animals. Cyrus McCormick invented his reaping machine in America, heralding a new age of mechanized harvesting.

Ideas

As might be expected in a time of such ferment, the century was rich in philosophers, though the ideas that had, and continue to have, the most impact came from other quarters. Philosophically, the high ground was held by the Germans, much as the French had held it in the previous century. The great names of the Beethoven era included Hegel (1770–1831) and Schopenhauer (1788–1860), both of whom were much concerned with music in one way or another. Hegel argued that consciousness and the world of external objects were inseparable aspects of a single whole, and that truth is discoverable only through a dialectic process of contradiction and resolution—a thoroughly rationalist idea with clear parallels in the concept of sonata form (see Glossary). Schopenhauer took a more pessimistic view (and one more in keeping with the preoccupations of the Romantics), in which the irrational will is seen as the governing principle of our perception, dominated by an endless cycle of desire and frustration from which the only escape is aesthetic contemplation. His thinking was to have a powerful effect on both Wagner and Nietzsche, who rejected established concepts of Christian morality. Nietzsche proclaimed that "God is dead" and postulated the ideal of the *Übermensch* ("Superman"), who would impose his self-created will on the weak and the worthless. This view was fully in keeping with the gargantuan nature of the Romantic ego, with its roots in the controlling powers of the Industrial Revolution and the spate of scientific discoveries that granted Man an ever greater mastery of his environment.

Literature

In the realm of literature this was the century of the novel, pioneered in England by Jane Austen and Sir Walter Scott, and in Germany by Goethe, "Jean Paul" (J.P.F. Richter), and the fantastical E.T.A. Hoffmann (whose critical writings on Beethoven are among the most perceptive ever penned).

Architecture

Nineteenth-century architecture in Europe and America reflected both the Romantic obsession with the past and the industrialists' concerns with practicality and economy. Public buildings tended for most of the century towards an ever more massive grandiosity, drawing on a wide variety of styles ranging from the distant to the recent past, often within a single building. A famous example is the Palace of Westminster (better known as the Houses of Parliament) in London.

Music

Never has an art known greater changes in so relatively short a time than music in the nineteenth century. When the century began, Beethoven was only twenty-nine, Schubert barely three. Haydn, at sixty-seven, was still at the height of his powers. When it ended, Debussy's revolutionary *Prélude à l'après-midi d'un faune*, often cited, even today, as "the beginning of modern music," was already seven years old, and Schoenberg (twenty-five), Ives (also twenty-five), Bartók (eighteen), and Stravinsky (seventeen) were all fully active. In between, the end of the Classical era and the dawning of Romanticism could be seen in the maturest works of Beethoven and Schubert (whose symphonies, sonatas, and chamber music expanded Classical forms to previously undreamt-of proportions); harmony underwent unprecedented transformations, including the progressive dissolution of traditional tonality by Liszt, Wagner, Debussy, Mahler, and Ives (for more on tonality, see Glossary); the piano attained its full maturity (its evolution significantly dominated by the influence of Beethoven and Liszt) and became the world's most popular instrument; and the art of orchestration became a frontline issue, thanks in no small part to Beethoven's symphonies, overtures, and concertos. There was a major shift from the relative "objectivity" of the Classical era to the intensely emotional outpourings of the Romantics. Illustrative, "program" music achieved a popularity never approached before or since, and the cult of virtuosity became a dominant feature. The specialist (i.e., non-composing) performer became the rule rather than the exception and musical schools and conservatories became commonplace.

Despite this, the discipline of counterpoint, hitherto amongst the most highly prized of musical attributes, fell into widespread disuse (though it plays an important part in Beethoven's music, as it was later to do in that of Liszt, Bruckner, Wagner, Brahms, and Richard Strauss). In the works of Schubert, Lanner, Weber, and the Strauss family, the waltz became the most popular form of the century. Forms in general polarized, from the millions of piano miniatures and "character pieces," to the gargantuan music dramas of Wagner, the sprawling symphonies of Bruckner and Mahler, and the extravagantly colored symphonic works of Richard Strauss.

Personalities

Albrechtsberger, Johann Georg (1736–1809): Esteemed German organist, composer, and pedagogue, best remembered today for having instructed Beethoven in counterpoint during Haydn's absence in London.

Bach, Carl Philipp Emanuel (1714–1788): Second surviving son of J.S. Bach. One of the foremost composers and harpsichordists of his day, his works were highly influential in effecting the transition from the High Baroque to the Classical era. His *Essay on the True Art of Playing Keyboard Instruments* (1753), still widely read today, was recommended by Beethoven to the young Czerny.

Brentano, Antonie (*née* von Birkenstock) (1780–1869): Wife of Franz Brentano from Frankfurt. The family visited Vienna from 1809 to 1812, and Antonie was almost certainly the "Immortal Beloved" of Beethoven's famous unsent letter. Eleven years later he dedicated the "Diabelli" Variations to her.

Brentano, Bettina (1785–1859): Half-sister of Franz, she married the poet Achim von Arnim in 1811. A poet herself, she was instrumental in introducing Beethoven to Goethe.

Brentano, Maximiliane (1802–1861): Daughter of Franz and Antonie, for whom Beethoven composed the one-movement Trio in B flat, WoO39 in 1812 (the same year as the letter to her mother) "for the encouragement of her piano-playing." Also dedicated to her is the Piano Sonata in E, Op. 109.

Bridgetower, George (1778–1860): Violinist (son of an African father and Polish mother) who met Beethoven in Vienna and Teplitz and gave the first performance with him of the famous "Kreutzer" Sonata in 1803.

Cherubini, Maria Luigi (1760–1842): Italian composer, resident in Paris from 1778. In 1822 he was appointed director of the Paris Conservatoire, and was greatly admired by Beethoven, who preferred Cherubini's Requiem to Mozart's. Renowned for his gruff conservatism, he was amusingly (and unfairly) pilloried by Berlioz in his highly readable *Mémoires*.

Clementi, Muzio (1752–1832): Italian composer and virtuoso pianist. He pioneered a truly idiomatic piano style when the instrument was only just beginning to oust the harpsichord in public favor. A teacher of both Cramer and Field, he composed a celebrated book of pianistic studies, *Gradus ad Parnassum*, still widely used today.

Cramer, Johann Baptist (1771–1858): German pianist and composer. A pupil of Clementi, he too produced many studies for the piano, a number of which are still in use today and have considerable artistic merit. Beethoven is said to have admired him above all other pianists.

Czerny, Carl (1791–1857): Austrian pianist and composer, a pupil of Hummel, Clementi, and Beethoven, and the teacher of Liszt. Astoundingly prolific, he had several writing desks in his study, each supporting a different work in progress. While the ink dried on one, he moved on to the next, thus becoming music's first one-man assembly line. His many studies have driven countless piano students to distraction.

Deym, Countess Josephine (*née* Brunsvik) (1779–1821): She took lessons from Beethoven along with her sister Therese before marrying Count Deym in 1799. After the Count's death in 1804 she formed a close relationship with Beethoven, who was clearly in love with her and hoped to marry her. She left Vienna with her family in 1808 and married Baron von Stackelberg two years later.

Diabelli, Anton (1781–1858): Minor composer and publisher. It was on a slight and nondescript waltz by Diabelli that Beethoven based his monumental "Diabelli" Variations, Op. 120.

Fétis, François-Joseph (1784–1871): French composer, musicologist, and critic. A professor at the Paris Conservatoire from 1821, he became its librarian in 1827. His *Biographie universelle des musiciens* was an important forerunner of *Grove's Dictionary of Music and Musicians*, and his *Histoire générale de la musique* is still a valuable reference book for scholars.

Galitsin, Prince Nikolas (1794–1860): Amateur cellist and musical enthusiast from St Petersburg. In 1822 he commissioned Beethoven to write some more string quartets, and Op. 127, Op. 130, and Op. 132 were dedicated to him. He also organized the first complete performance of the *Missa solemnis*, which was given in St Petersburg in April 1824.

Gelinek, Abbé Joseph (1758–1825): Bohemian pianist, composer, and priest, who became chaplain and piano teacher to Prince Kinsky in 1786 and to the Esterházy household from 1795. He met Beethoven in Vienna in 1793 and was overwhelmed by his brilliant improvisations, just as he was beaten by him in a pianistic duel.

Goethe, Johann Wolfgang von (1749–1832): German poet, dramatist, scientist, and courtier. The most renowned of all German writers, his works had an incalculable effect on the birth and early development of the Romantic movement. Beethoven made more settings of Goethe than of any other poet.

Hiller, Ferdinand von (1811–1885): German composer, conductor, and teacher. A child prodigy, he was taken by Hummel to visit the dying Beethoven.

Hummel, Johann Nepomuk (1778–1837): German-Hungarian pianist and composer, studied with Mozart and Clementi, taught Czerny and Thalberg, and was ranked in his day only just below Mozart and Beethoven. As a pianist he was considered supreme between the death of Mozart and the emergence of Liszt, Chopin, and Thalberg.

Kant, Immanuel (1724–1804): Highly influential German philosopher much admired by Beethoven, who possessed some of his works. Extracts from his *Allgemeine Naturgeschichte* were copied out in Beethoven's *Tagebuch* of 1812–18.

Kinsky, Prince Ferdinand (1781–1812): A patron of Beethoven's and the major contributor to the annuity agreed with the Archduke Rudolph and Prince Lobkowitz in 1809. He was killed in a riding accident in November 1812.

Kotzebue, August von (1761–1819): Popular German poet and dramatist. Beethoven wrote the overtures and incidental music for his plays *The Ruins of Athens* and *King Stephen*, to celebrate the opening of a new theatre in Pest in 1812.

Kozeluch, Leopold (1747–1818): Bohemian composer. He settled in Vienna in 1778 and became a popular piano teacher of the aristocracy. He was a versatile and prolific composer, especially of symphonies and piano music, and, like Haydn, Pleyel, and Beethoven, arranged Scottish airs for Thomson of Edinburgh.

Kreutzer, Rodolphe (1766–1831): French violinist and composer. He met Beethoven in Vienna in 1798, and was later the dedicatee of the Violin Sonata in A, Op. 47, which has ever since borne his name.

Lenz, Wilhelm von (1809–1883): Russian writer on music, of German descent. It was he who first divided Beethoven's work into three chronological periods. In Paris he had piano lessons from both Chopin and Liszt, and his book *The Great Pianists of Our Time* (1872) is an absorbing (if unreliable) source of information on the subject.

Lichnowsky, Prince Karl von (1756–1814): A pupil and patron of Mozart, he became Beethoven's first benefactor in Vienna, invited him to live in his apartment, and granted him an annuity from 1800 onwards. He received several important dedications, beginning with the Op. 1 piano trios, which were first performed at his house.

Lichnowsky, Count Moritz von (1771–1837): Younger brother of the above, he also became a great admirer of Beethoven, who composed the two-movement Piano Sonata, Op. 90 for him, humorously connecting its changing moods to the Count's forthcoming marriage to a singer.

Lobkowitz, Prince Franz Joseph (1772–1816): One of Beethoven's most important patrons, he was among the three noblemen who granted him an annuity in 1809 in a successful attempt to prevent his emigration from Vienna. His private orchestra gave the first performance of the "Eroica" Symphony in his palace. The work was later dedicated to him.

Malfatti, Dr Giovanni (1775–1859): Esteemed Italian-born doctor. It was he who suggested that Beethoven take the waters at Teplitz and attended him in his final illness. His niece Therese was among the many women who spurned Beethoven as a suitor, describing him even in his early manhood as ugly and "half mad."

Mälzel, Johann Nepomuk (1772–1838): Best known for his invention of the metronome. It was for his mechanical orchestra, the Panharmonicon, that Beethoven originally composed his "Battle" Symphony in 1813.

Moscheles, Ignaz (1794–1870): Famous Czech-born pianist, conductor, and composer. He was an early champion of Beethoven's piano works and later became his friend.

Neefe, Christian Gottlob (1748–1798): Beethoven's first important teacher, he studied law at Leipzig but soon abandoned it for music. As a composer of Singspielen he came to Bonn in 1779 to direct the music for Grossman's theatrical company, but was appointed court organist in 1781.

Pleyel, Ignaz Josef (1757–1831): Austrian composer and publisher, pupil of Haydn. He later moved to Strassburg (modern-day Strasbourg) and London, and settled in Paris, where he founded a famous firm of piano-makers and publishers in 1807. He returned to Vienna and had several meetings with Beethoven in 1805.

Razumovsky, Count (later Prince) Andrey (1752–1836): Russian ambassador in Vienna from 1792. He was a keen amateur violinist, and commissioned from Beethoven the three string quartets, Op. 59, which still bear his name.

Reicha, Antonín (Antoine) (1770–1836): Bohemian composer, violinist, pianist, and teacher. He was among the first to experiment with polytonality (music in two keys simultaneously), and knew Beethoven in his Bonn days, when they were both members of the Electoral Orchestra in which Beethoven played the viola.

Ries, Ferdinand (1784–1838): German composer and pianist who studied the piano with Beethoven in the early 1800s and helped to compile the first collection of biographical documents relating to his life.

Rudolph, Archduke (1788–1831): Son of Emperor Leopold II and an accomplished composer and pianist. He studied with

Beethoven from 1803 and became one of his most esteemed and lasting friends and patrons, a fact reflected in the large number of important works which Beethoven dedicated to him.

Salieri, Antonio (1750–1825): Prolific Italian-born opera composer, best known today as the jealous rival of Mozart, as related in the play and film *Amadeus*. He was one of the very few teachers whom Beethoven greatly admired, and with whom he studied, on and off, for many years after his move to Vienna in 1792.

Schindler, Anton (1795–1864): Moravian-born law-student-turned-violinist. He became Beethoven's friend and general drudge after 1814 and was among his first and most unreliable biographers.

Schuppanzigh, Ignaz (1776–1830): Notably corpulent Austrian violinist and conductor, whose girth made him the frequent butt of Beethoven's indelicate jokes. Closely associated with Beethoven's music from the mid-1790s onwards, he is thought also to have given him violin lessons. As leader of various string quartets, he supervised the first performances of most of Beethoven's works in that medium.

Seyfried, Ignaz Ritter von (1776–1841): Composer and fellow pupil of Albrechtsberger. Knew Beethoven over a long period and contributed a number of interesting recollections.

Simrock, Nicolaus (1750–1832): German horn player and later a famous music publisher. He issued the first editions of a number of Beethoven's most important works, including the "Kreutzer" Sonata and the late cello sonatas.

Spohr, Louis (1784–1859): Eminent composer, violinist, and conductor, resident in Vienna from 1812 to 1815. He was a memorable chronicler of Beethoven's eccentricities as a conductor.

Steibelt, Daniel (1765–1823): Minor German pianist and composer whose chief stock-in-trade was his arsenal of "shivering" tremolandos. He enjoyed widespread popularity for a number of years, though was regarded by musicians as something of a charlatan. After being spectacularly trounced by Beethoven in a pianistic "duel," he subsequently refused to attend any gathering at which Beethoven was likely to be present.

Swieten, Baron Gottfried van (1734–1803): Austrian diplomat, doctor, and amateur musician. A friend of Haydn, Mozart, and Beethoven, he was an enthusiastic scholar of "early" music and introduced many people, Haydn and Mozart included, to numerous works by Bach and Handel. Beethoven's Symphony No. 1 was dedicated to him.

Thomson, George (1757–1851): Scottish publisher and folksong collector who commissioned a number of composers, including Haydn and Beethoven, to write piano accompaniments with various *ad hoc* parts for other instruments.

Waldstein, Count Ferdinand von (1762–1823): One of Beethoven's early patrons in Bonn, he commissioned the *Ritterballett* (WoO1), Beethoven's first purely orchestral score, and in 1805 became the dedicatee of the Sonata in C, Op. 53, which has borne his name ever since.

Weber, Carl Maria von (1786–1826): Influential German composer. He was one of the foremost exponents of Romantic opera, foreshadowing Wagner. His most famous work, *Der Freischütz*, is still in the repertoire today.

Wölfl, Joseph (1773–1812): Pianist and composer, born in Salzburg where he studied with Leopold Mozart and Michael Haydn. Much esteemed as a piano virtuoso, he met Beethoven in Vienna in 1798 and dedicated some sonatas to him.

Selected Bibliography

Abraham, Gerald, ed., *The New Oxford History of Music*, Vol. VIII, "The Age of Beethoven," London, 1982

Anderson, Emily, ed. and trans., *The Letters of Beethoven*, London, 1961

Arnold, Denis, and Fortune, Nigel, eds, *The Beethoven Companion*, London, 1971

Breuning, Gerhard (ed. Maynard Solomon), *Memories of Beethoven*, Cambridge, 1992

Cooper, Barry, *Beethoven*, Oxford, 2000

Cooper, Barry, ed., *The Beethoven Compendium: A Guide to Beethoven's Life and Music*, London, 1996

Cooper, Martin, *Beethoven: The Last Decade, 1817–1827*, London, 1970

Czerny, Carl (ed. Paul Badura-Skoda), *On the Proper Performance of all Beethoven's Works for the Piano*, Vienna, 1970

Grove, Sir George, *Beethoven and his Nine Symphonies*, London, 1896, repr. 1962

Hamburger, Michael, ed. and trans., *Beethoven: Letters, Journals and Conversations*, New York, 1960

Hopkins, Antony, *The Nine Symphonies of Beethoven*, London, 1981

Kerman, Joseph, *The Beethoven Quartets*, New York, 1967

Kerman, Joseph, and Tyson, Alan, *The New Grove Beethoven*, London, 1983

Kinderman, William, *Beethoven*, Oxford and Berkeley, 1995

Landon, H.C. Robbins, *Beethoven: A Documentary Study*, London, 1970

Marliave, Joseph de, *Beethoven's Quartets*, Oxford, 1928, repr. 1961

Matthews, Denis, *Beethoven*, London, 1985

Newman, Ernest, *The Unconscious Beethoven*, London, 1927, repr. 1969

Plantinga, Leon, *Beethoven's Concertos*, New York and London, 1999

Rosen, Charles, *The Classical Style*, New York and London, 1971

Shedlock, J.S., trans., *Beethoven's Letters*, London, 1909, repr. 1972

Solomon, Maynard, *Beethoven*, New York, 1977

Solomon, Maynard, *Beethoven Essays*, Cambridge, 1986

Sonneck, O.G., ed., *Beethoven: Impressions of Contemporaries*, New York, 1926, repr. 1967

Sterba, Editha and Richard, *Beethoven and his Nephew*, New York, 1954

Sullivan, J.W.N., *Beethoven–His Spiritual Development*, London, 1927, repr. 1979

Tovey, D.F., *Essays in Musical Analysis*, London, 1935–44

Tovey, D.F., *Beethoven*, London, 1944

Tyson, Alan, ed., *Beethoven Studies*, New York, 1973, London, 1974

Glossary

Accelerando Getting faster.

Adagio Slow.

Alberti bass A stylized accompaniment popular in the later eighteenth century. It is based on the triad, "spelled out" in the order bottom–top–middle–top (as in C–G–E–G, etc.).

Allegretto Moderately fast, rather slower than *Allegro* and often lighter in tone.

Allegro Fast, but not excessively so.

Alto Term used to describe either a male falsetto or a low female voice. In a four-part choir the altos sing the second-highest line, between the sopranos and the tenors.

Andante Slowish, at a moderate walking pace.

Aria Solo song (also called "air"), generally as part of an opera or oratorio. It has a ternary (A–B–A) design in which the third part duplicates (and usually embellishes) the first, and is often called a "da capo" aria.

Arpeggio A chord spelled out, one note at a time, either from bottom to top or vice versa (C–E–G–C; F–A–C–F, etc.).

Articulation The joining together or separation of notes, to form specific groups. When notes are separated by slivers of silence, the effect is often of an intake of breath; and like the intake of breath before speech it heightens anticipation of what is to follow. When they are joined together, the effect is of words spoken in the expenditure of a single breath. See also "Legato" and "Staccato."

Augmentation The expansion of note-values, generally to twice their original length.

Bagatelle Literally "trifle." A short, light piece, often for piano. Beethoven wrote twenty-six, by no means all light or "trifling." His Six Bagatelles, Op. 126, include some of his profoundest and most moving music.

Bar (US: Measure) The visual division of meter into successive units, marked off on the page by vertical lines.

Bass The lowest part of the musical texture.

Beat The unit of pulse; the underlying "throb" of the music.

Bel canto Literally, "beautiful singing." Often used to describe a smooth, lyrical aria in which the expressive powers of the voice can be used to the full.

Binary A simple two-part form (A:B). Part one typically moves from the tonic (home key) to the dominant (secondary key), while part two moves from the dominant back to the tonic.

Cadence A coming to rest on a particular note or key, as in the standard "Amen" at the end of a hymn.

Cadenza A relatively brief, often showy solo of improvisatory character in the context of a concerto, operatic aria, or other orchestral form. In concertos, it usually heralds the orchestral close to a movement, generally the first.

Canon An imitative device like the common round (*Frère Jacques, Three Blind Mice, London's Burning*) in which the same tune comes in at staggered intervals of time.

Cantabile Song-like, singingly.

Cantata A work in several movements for accompanied voice or voices (from the Latin *cantare*, to sing).

Chord Any simultaneous combination of three or more notes. Chords are analogous to words, just as the notes of which they consist are analogous to letters.

Chromatic Notes (and the using of notes) that are not contained in the standard "diatonic" scales that form the basis of most western music. In the scale of C major (which uses only the white keys of the piano), every black key is "chromatic."

Coda The "tailpiece" at the end of a sonata-form movement. In Haydn and Mozart the coda is often no more than a brief flourish. Many of Beethoven's codas are long and elaborate, and involve further thematic development.

Codetta A small coda, usually at the end of the exposition in a sonata-form movement.

Concerto A work usually for solo instrument and orchestra, generally in three movements (fast–slow–fast).

Continuo A form of accompaniment in the seventeenth and eighteenth centuries, in which a keyboard instrument, usually a harpsichord, harmonizes the bass line played by the cello.

Contrapuntal	See "Counterpoint."
Counterpoint	The interweaving of separate "horizontal" melodic lines, as opposed to the accompaniment of a top-line ("horizontal") melody by a series of "vertical" chords.
Crescendo	Getting louder.
Cross-rhythms	See "Polyrhythm."
Development section	The middle section in a sonata-form movement, normally characterized by movement through several keys.
Diatonic	Using only the scale-steps of the prevailing key notes of the regular scale.
Diminuendo	Getting softer.
Diminution	The contraction of note-values, normally to half their original length.
Dotted rhythm	A "jagged" pattern of sharply distinguished longer and shorter notes, the long, accented note being followed by a short, unaccented one, or the other way round. Examples are the openings of the *Marseillaise, The Star-Spangled Banner,* and, even better, *The Battle Hymn of the Republic:* "Mine eyes have seen the glory of the coming of the Lord."
Double-stopping	The playing of two notes simultaneously on a stringed instrument.
Duple rhythm	Any rhythm based on units of two beats, or multiples thereof.
Dynamics	The gradations of softness and loudness, and the terms that indicate them (*pianissimo, fortissimo.* etc.).
Exposition	The first section in a piece in sonata form, in which the main themes and their relationships are first presented.
Fantasy, fantasia	A free form, often of an improvisatory nature, following the composer's fancy rather than any preordained structures. But there are some fantasies, like Schubert's *Wanderer Fantasy* and Schumann's Fantasy in C for the piano, which are tightly integrated works incorporating fully fledged sonata forms, scherzos, fugal sections, etc.
Finale	A generic term for "last movement."
Flat	A note lowered by a semitone from its "natural" position.
Forte, fortissimo	Loud, very loud.

Fugue An imitative work in several overlapping parts or "voices" (the term applies regardless of whether the fugue is vocal or instrumental). Fugue derives from the same principle as the common round, though it can be immeasurably more complicated. More of a technique than a fixed form, it begins with a solo tune (known as the "subject"). On the completion of this tune (or melodic fragment–there are some fugues based on a mere four notes), the second voice enters with an "answer" (the same tune, but in a different, complementary key). While the second voice is presenting the theme ("subject"), the first continues with a new tune (known as a "countersubject"). In the overlapping scheme of things this is equivalent to the second phrase of a round or canon ("Dormez-vous?" in *Frère Jacques,* "See how they run" in *Three Blind Mice*). When subject and countersubject complete their dovetailed counterpoint, another "voice" enters with its own statement of the subject. Voice two now repeats voice one's countersubject, while voice one introduces a new countersubject. And so it goes, alternating with "episodes" in which the various voices combine in free counterpoint, but with no full statements of the subject in any voice.

Fortepiano The name given to the early pianos known to Mozart. Their sound is similar to a cross between a harpsichord and a harp.

Glissando Literally "gliding"; a sliding between any two notes, producing something of a "siren" effect.

Harmony The simultaneous sounding of notes to make a chord. Harmonies (chords) often serve as expressive or atmospheric "adjectives," describing or giving added meaning to the notes of a melody, which, in turn, might be likened to nouns and verbs.

Harpsichord A keyboard instrument in which the strings are plucked rather than struck.

Homophony When all parts move at once, giving the effect of a melody (the top line) accompanied by chords.

Interval The distance in pitch between two notes, heard either simultaneously or successively. The sounding of the first two notes of a scale is therefore described as a major or minor "second," the sounding of the first and third notes a major or minor third, etc.

Key See "Tonality."

Largo Slow, broad, serious.

Legato Literally "bound." A smooth, seamless vocal or instrumental line. The opposite of *staccato.*

Lied (plural Lieder)	German for "song." The term is typically used for a song with piano accompaniment by nineteenth- and early twentieth-century composers, most famously Beethoven, Schubert, Schumann, Brahms, Wolf, and Richard Strauss.
Major	See "Modes."
Measure	See "Bar."
Meter, metrical	The grouping together of beats in recurrent units of two, three, four, six, etc. Meter is the pulse of music.
Minor	See "Modes."
Modes	The names given to the particular arrangement of notes within a scale. Every key in western classical music has two versions, the major and the minor mode; the decisive factor is the size of the interval between the key note (the tonic, the foundation on which scales are built) and the third degree of the scale; if it is compounded of two whole tones (as in C–E), the mode is major; if the third tone is made up of one and a half tones (C to E flat), the mode is minor. In general, the minor mode is darker, more "serious," more moody, more obviously dramatic than the major. The church modes prevalent in the Middle Ages comprise various combinations of major and minor and are less dynamically "directed" in character. These have appeared only rarely in music since the Baroque (c. 1600–1750) and have generally been used by composers to create some kind of archaic effect.
Modulate, modulation	The movement from one key to another, generally involving at least one pivotal chord common to both keys.
Motif, motive	A motif can be seen as a kind of musical acorn. It is a melodic/rhythmic figure too brief to constitute a proper theme, but one on which themes are built; a perfect example is the beginning of Beethoven's Fifth Symphony: ta–ta–ta–*dah*; ta–ta–ta–*dah*.
Natural	Not sharp or flat.
Nocturne	The Romantic keyboard nocturne was "invented" by the Irish composer John Field and exalted by Chopin. Cast in a simple ternary (A–B–A) form, its outer sections consist of a long-spun melody of a generally "dreamy" sort, supported by a flowing, arpeggio-based accompaniment. The middle section, in some ways analogous to the development section in sonata form, is normally more turbulent and harmonically unstable.

Octave	The simultaneous sounding of any note with its nearest namesake, up or down (C to C, F to F, etc.); the effect is an enrichment, through increased mass and variety of pitch, of either note as sounded by itself.
Oratorio	An extended but unstaged setting of a religious text in narrative/dramatic form, usually for soloists, chorus, and orchestra. The most famous example is Handel's *Messiah*.
Phrase	A smallish group of notes (generally accommodated by the exhalation of a single breath) that form a unit of melody, as in "God save our Gracious Queen" and "My Country, 'tis of thee."
Phrasing	The shaping of music into phrases.
Piano, pianissimo	Soft, very soft.
Pianoforte	The full name of the piano, now regarded as archaic, as in "violoncello" for the cello.
Pizzicato	Plucked strings.
Polyphony	Music with interweaving parts.
Polyrhythm	The superposition of different rhythms or meters.
Prelude	Literally, a piece that precedes and introduces another piece (as in the standard "Prelude and Fugue"). However, the name has been applied (most famously by Bach, Chopin, and Debussy) to describe freestanding short pieces, often of a semi-improvisatory nature.
Presto	Very fast.
Program music	Illustrative music, music that tells a story.
Recapitulation	The third section in sonata form (see below), where the ideas of the exposition return in the home key. Recapitulations often also involve fresh thematic development.
Recitative	A short narrative section especially characteristic of Baroque and Classical opera and oratorio. It is normally sung by a solo voice accompanied by continuo chords, and usually precedes an aria. The rhythm is in a free style, being dictated by the words.
Resolution	When a suspension or dissonance comes to rest.
Rest	A measured "silence" (or, to be more accurate, a suspension of sound) in an instrumental or vocal part.

Rhythm   That aspect of music concerned with duration and accent. Notes may be of many contrasting lengths and derive much of their character and definition from patterns of accentuation and emphasis determined by the composer.

Ritardando,   Getting slower.
ritenuto

Ritornello   A theme or section for orchestra recurring in different keys between solo passages in an aria or concerto.

Rondo   A movement in which the main theme announced at the beginning makes repeated appearances, interspersed with contrasting sections known as "episodes." At its simplest (when the episodes are more or less identical) the form can be summarized by the formula A–B–A–B–A. In most rondos, though, the episodes are different in each case: A–B–A–C–A. There are also many rondos with more episodes (A–B–A–C–A–D–A etc.). The form appears both as a self-contained work in its own right and as a movement (usually the last) of a sonata, symphony, or concerto.

Scale   From the Italian word *scala* ("ladder"). A series of adjacent, "stepwise" notes (A–B–C–D, etc.), moving up or down. These "ladders" provide the basic cast of characters from which melodies are made and keys established.

Sharp   A note raised by a semitone from its "natural" position.

Singspiel   An opera, usually comic and in German with spoken dialogue.

Sonata form   Also known as "sonata-allegro" and "first-movement" form, this was the dominant form throughout the second half of the eighteenth century and the first third of the nineteenth. It is basically a ternary (three-part) design in which the last part is a repeat of the first (as in the *da capo* aria), but with one very important difference: while the first section is cast in two contrasting keys, the third remains largely, and ends, in the key of the tonic (the key of the movement as a whole).

The three sections of the standard sonata form are called exposition, development, and recapitulation. The exposition, which may be prefaced by a slow introduction, is based on the complementary tensions of two "opposing" keys. Each key-group generally has its own themes, but this contrast is of secondary importance (many of Haydn's sonata movements are based on a single theme, which passes through various adventures on its voyages from key to key). In movements in the major mode, the secondary key is almost invariably the dominant. When the key of the movement is in the minor mode, the secondary key will almost always be the relative major. The exposition always ends in the secondary key, never in the tonic.

In many sonata-form movements, the main themes of the two key-groups will also be of a contrasting character. If the first main theme is blustery or military, the second, in the complementary key, is likely to be more lyrical.

The development is altogether more free and unpredictable. In most cases, true to its name, it takes themes or ideas from the exposition and "develops" them; or it may ignore the themes of the exposition altogether, as Mozart often does. What it will have is a notably increased sense of harmonic instability, drifting, or in some cases struggling, through a number of different keys before delivering us back to the tonic for the recapitulation. Since the recapitulation lacks the tonal tensions of the exposition (though it may contain further development), the themes themselves, now generally in the tonic key, take on a new relationship. In many of Beethoven's works, the recapitulation is followed by a substantial coda. In its prescribed resolution of family (tonal) conflicts, sonata form may be seen as the most Utopian of all musical structures.

Sonata — Usually a piece for solo piano, or one instrument plus piano, in three movements. The overall layout consists of a fast (or quite fast) opening movement (normally in sonata form), a central slow movement, and a quick finale (often a rondo). Sometimes there are four movements, in which case the extra one is almost always a minuet or (from Beethoven onwards) a scherzo, and the finale either in rondo or sonata form.

String quartet — A sonata for two violins, viola, and cello, normally in four movements; also the name for the instrumental group itself.

String quintet — A sonata normally for string quartet with an additional viola or (infrequently) an additional cello. It is usually in four movements.

Staccato — Detached, the opposite of *legato*.

Suspension — A note from one chord held over into a following chord of which it is not a member. The result is almost always a heightening of emotional intensity.

Symphony — A sonata for orchestra.

Syncopation — Accents falling on irregular beats, generally giving a "swinging" feel, as in much of jazz.

Tempo — The speed of music.

Ternary — A three-part form in which the third part is a repeat of the first (A–B–A).

Tonality	There is probably no aspect of music harder to describe than tonality or "key." Put at its broadest, it has to do with a kind of tonal solar system in which each note ("planet"), each rung of the scale (from *scala*, the Italian word for "ladder"), exists in a fixed and specific relationship to one particular note ("sun"), which is known as the "key note" or "tonic." When this planetary system is based on the note "C," the music is said to be "in" the key of C. Each note of the scale has a different state of "tension," a different degree of "unrest" in relation to the key note. And each arouses a different degree of expectation in the listener, which the composer can either resolve or frustrate. Through the use of "alien" notes, not present in the prevailing scale, the composer can shift from one solar system, from one key, to another. On the way, a sense of stability gives way to a sense of instability, of flux, that is not resolved until the arrival of the new key. This process of moving from one key to another is known as "modulation."
Tone color, timbre	That property of sound that distinguishes a horn from a piano, a violin from a xylophone, etc.
Tone painting	The use of instrumental "color" to imitate or evoke natural and other sounds (birdsong, the hunt, the spinning wheel, etc.).
Tremolo, tremolando	From the Italian for "trembling" or "shaking," a tremolo is a rapid reiteration of a single note through back-and-forth movements of the bow, or the rapid and repeated alternation of two notes.
Triad	A three-note chord, especially those including the root, third, and fifth of a scale (C–E–G, A–C–E, etc.) in any order.
Triplets	In duple meter, a grouping (or groupings) of three notes in the space of two (as in the "Buckle-my" of "One-two / Buckle-my-shoe").
Una corda	Literally "one string," *una corda* denotes the use of the soft pedal on the piano.
Unison	The simultaneous sounding of a single note by more than one singer or player, as in the congregational singing of a hymn.
Variation	Any decorative or otherwise purposeful alteration of a note, rhythm, timbre, etc.
Vibrato	A rapid, regular fluctuation in pitch, giving the note a "throbbing" effect.
Vivace, vivacissimo	Fast and lively, extremely fast and lively.

Annotations of CD Tracks

Compiling a program of works that complement and amplify the text presented a dilemma. The length of many of Beethoven's greatest works, generally dominated by his first and slow movements, has resulted here in a disproportionate number of finales since these, in most cases, are the shortest. To opt for longer movements would be to opt for fewer works, thereby weakening the variety essential to a fully rounded portrait of the man. Since the aim of this CD sequence is biographical rather than artistic, shorter movements have tended to prevail.

CD 1

1 Piano Concerto No. 2 in B flat, Op. 19. Finale: Rondo. Molto allegro

Disregarding a work from his boyhood, for which we have only the piano part and a few orchestral cues, Beethoven's "Second" Piano Concerto is actually his first (the numbering reflects only the order of publication). Possibly begun as early as 1788, it was revised several times, not reaching its final form until 1798 (if indeed even then— the piano part was first written out in 1801). Could the young titan have been intimidated by the example of Mozart, whose twenty-three piano concertos set a standard for the form that has never been surpassed? Even after its various revisions, the B flat Concerto is the most "Mozartian" in Beethoven's output, but the individuality of its composer is never in doubt. Typically Beethovenian is the rhythmic jokiness of this finale, where he deliberately tries to confuse the listener's perception of the meter. Typical, too, is the ebullient good humor of the movement as a whole.

2 Piano Trio in C minor, Op. 1 No. 3. Finale: Prestissimo

Beethoven's first major chamber works were the three piano trios, Op. 1 (piano, violin, and cello). Even here, at the formal beginning of his career as a composer, he was a master wholly fit to stand beside his teacher Haydn. Quite apart from their mastery, however, they are notable for their emancipation of the cello, which in Haydn's trios seldom does more than double the left hand of the piano part. Also significant is Beethoven's adoption of the spacious four-movement plan normally associated with the Classical symphony—a plan chosen for all but one of his subsequent trios. The last of the Op. 1 set, in C minor, is notable for being the most intensely emotional and dramatic piano trio written to date. With its many bold gestures, powerful accents and sharp dynamic contrasts, it alarmed Haydn, who feared—wrongly as it turned out—that it would be misunderstood by the Viennese. The features that so disturbed Haydn became hallmarks of Beethoven's style.

3 Symphony No. 1 in C, Op. 21. **Finale: Adagio—Allegro molto e vivace**

Beethoven delayed writing his First Symphony until his thirtieth year. From an early age, he felt a powerful sense of destiny, complemented by a brashly competitive streak. He knew that when he tackled the symphony he must be brave enough, and sufficiently well-armed, to confront the awesome examples of Mozart and Haydn head-on. With the very opening of his First Symphony he not only declares himself ready but openly mocks the expectations of his audience. He starts with a lone, two-chord cadence—the standard formula for ending a piece, not beginning one—and he does it in the wrong key. Three bars later he is still in cadential mode, and still in the wrong key (but now a different one). And at the start of the last movement, he plays out the notes of an ascending scale one by one ("Wait for it, folks!"), each new step arousing a different degree of expectation. No composer ever got more artistic mileage out of the frustration of expectation than Beethoven.

4 Piano Sonata No. 8 in C minor, Op. 13 "Pathétique"
Movement 1: Grave—Allegro di molto e con brio

The "Pathétique" Sonata, Op. 13, always among Beethoven's most popular works, finds him drawing on symphonic models (and Haydn's symphonies in particular) in its use of a substantial slow introduction. The powerful, dramatic opening movement is the first in which Beethoven made significant alterations to the formal design of the Classical "sonata form." Repeatedly, at strategically placed moments, he brings back the slow introduction (or substantial, fragmentary developments of it). With its beautiful, long-spun melody, the slow movement reminds us that Beethoven was not only a highly dramatic but also a profoundly lyrical composer, whose big, singing tone at the piano was remarked on by everyone who heard him. The last movement is a rondo, in which the main theme and its several repetitions are interspersed with contrasting "episodes." A typically Beethovenian feature is the way in which much of the sonata derives from its opening bars.

[5] Symphony No. 3 in E flat, Op. 55 "Eroica." **Movement 2: Marcia funebre**

With the Third Symphony, the "Eroica" (1803), we come to one of the most revolutionary works in the history of art. Here the expansionism evident in the finale of the Second Symphony is extended to the entire work, which is roughly twice as long as the First and half again as long as any symphony then written. The scale is gigantic, the form monumental, the demands on the players unprecedented. In addition to its epic reach, much of the detail along the way is of a complexity and originality for which no one was prepared. If the Second Symphony represented the swansong of the Classical symphony, the Third may be said to have ushered in a new age. Nowhere is the work's monumentality more imposing than in the huge slow movement, the "Funeral March for a Dead Hero," inspired by the work's original dedicatee Napoleon Bonaparte. Beethoven violently repudiated him after he declared himself Emperor in 1804.

[6] Piano Sonata No. 23 in F minor, Op. 57 "Appassionata"
Finale: Allegro ma non troppo—Presto

The most famous sonatas of Beethoven's middle years are the ever-popular "Moonlight" (not Beethoven's term), the great C major, Op. 53 (known today as the "Waldstein," after its dedicatee Count Waldstein) and the still greater "Appassionata," Op. 57. Between them, they raised virtuosity to new heights. The aptly nicknamed "Appassionata" is an example, unique in its day, of almost unmitigated tragedy. Never before had the piano been entrusted with so much tumultuous emotion or such sustained tragic power (all the more affecting for the poignant beauty of the slow movement, whose repose is ripped apart by a single, shattering chord that leads straight into the almost shocking intensity of the final, doomed struggle). The conception of the work coincided with Beethoven's first awareness that he was going deaf. Here, more than in any of his earlier sonatas, Beethoven was writing beyond the capacities not only of most pianists but of the piano itself–thus forcing the pace of the instrument's evolution. Such powerful, sustained, even brutal assaults posed challenges to contemporary piano-makers that were not fully surmounted until well after Beethoven's death.

7 Symphony No. 2 in D, Op. 36. **Finale: Allegro molto**

In the exuberant Second Symphony (1802), no less than the First, Beethoven delights in foiling the listener's expectations. Here, though, he works on an altogether bigger scale. In the third movement, remembering that his adopted title "Scherzo" is the Italian word for joke, he makes a big show of obsessive repetition. But his biggest surprise of all is in the final movement. Everything about the symphony so far has suggested that Beethoven is conforming to the pattern of Haydn's late symphonies by following two extensive movements with two relatively brief ones. But just when we expect him to be winding up for the close, he goes sailing into a coda (literally "tailpiece") that eventually accounts for a third of the movement.

8 Fidelio, Op. 72. **Act II, No. 14: Quartet "Er sterbe!"**

Pizarro has ordered Rocco to kill Florestan before Don Fernando, the minister, arrives to inspect the prison. Rocco refuses. Pizarro himself will do it, but he orders Rocco to dig the grave, in the very dungeon where Florestan is imprisoned. Leonore, overhearing these arrangements, persuades the jailer Rocco to take her as his assistant. Rocco enters with the "boy" and orders her to help him dig a grave. In her anxiety to identify the prisoner, she nearly betrays herself, and can hardly suppress her emotion on recognizing her husband's voice. At the opening of the climactic quartet Pizarro arrives and tells Florestan he will kill him. Leonore defends him, crying out: "First kill his wife!" Florestan's rapture and Pizarro's rage burst out uncontrolled; Pizarro exclaims: "Shall I tremble before a woman?" and tries to murder both. Leonore, at bay, draws a pistol and retaliates: "One word more and you are dead"–when suddenly the sound of a distant trumpet strikes all else to silence. Don Fernando, the minister, has arrived; Florestan is saved. It is one of the great moments in opera.

9 | "Razumovsky" String Quartet in E minor, Op. 59 No. 2
Movement 3: Allegretto

Beethoven's sense of humor seldom deserted him, even in his most serious works. He loved musical jokes and he took an almost perverse pleasure in his ability to manipulate the feelings of his listeners. Who else would start the finale of an E minor quartet in the key of C major, and allow that key to pervade the movement as a whole? In this same work, Op. 59 No. 2, he jollies up the tense, distinctly un-jolly *Allegretto* third movement (which is neither a minuet nor a scherzo) by introducing a Russian folk tune in the "trio" section. He then worries away at it, with a repetitiousness that borders on parody, in a series of canonic imitations that refuse to get off the ground.

10 | Violin Concerto in D, Op. 61. Finale: Rondo

Beethoven's Violin Concerto is perhaps the most serenely Olympian concerto ever written. With its soaring lyricism and its panoramic perspective, it might almost be described as a three-movement symphony for violin and orchestra. Two things, however, disqualify it for that particular honor. One is the pervasive dialogue between violin and orchestra (there is nothing "embedded" about *this* soloist), the other is the form and character of the last movement. Like many concerto finales it is a rondo, in which recurrent appearances of the main theme are separated by contrasting "episodes." It is also of a very different character from the preceding two movements: playful, obtrusive, sometimes even jokey (the two pizzicato notes in one of the violin's returns, for example), and it features, in the first episode, the only example of out-and-out virtuosity in the whole concerto. True, the sky darkens briefly in episode 2 (in G minor), but nobody is fooled into thinking that the mood of the movement will turn tragic. Typical of Beethoven, and apt for the finale of this concerto, is the scale of the coda, which is larger than any previous section of the movement.

CD 2

[1] Piano Concerto No. 4 in G, Op. 58. **Movement 2: Andante con moto**

In the dramatic landscape that is Beethoven's middle period, the G major Piano Concerto occupies a very special place. Containing neither despair nor heroic struggle, it could easily be mistaken for a musical evocation of the Elysian Fields. The only hint of darkness is in the slow movement, where stark unison phrases in the orchestra provoke a gentle, pleading response from the piano. Beethoven's nineteenth-century biographer A.B. Marx famously compared this movement to Orpheus's taming of the Furies, and unlike many fanciful programmatic interpretations this one is remarkably true to the content of the music. During the course of the movement the orchestra's sternness is gradually appeased by the soloist's increasingly eloquent pleas. Finally, after an impassioned cadenza, the brusque unisons are reduced to a ghostly whisper in the basses.

[2] Symphony No. 5 in C minor, Op. 67. **Finale: Allegro**

Broadly speaking, Beethoven's themes fall into two categories. On the one hand there are the beautiful, long-spun melodies, often hymnlike in character; on the other there are short, motto-like figures that are more interesting for what happens to them than for themselves. A perfect case in point is the opening of the famous Fifth Symphony (1808). Dot–dot–dot–DASH–silence–Dot–dot–dot–DASH. A theme, yes; a tune, no. But from such acorns do Beethovenian oaks often grow. A remarkable amount of the first movement, and the scherzo and finale, too, derives in one way or another from this characteristically terse and unremarkable idea. For edge-of-the-seat excitement and adventure in music, the Fifth Symphony takes the cake. As millions of listeners have discovered, one needs no musical "knowledge" whatever to recognize in this work the triumph of the will over adversity. Starting with all the trappings of tragedy, it ends up as one of the most overpoweringly positive works ever conceived.

[3] Piano Trio in B flat, Op. 97 "Archduke"
Movement 3: Andante cantabile ma pero con moto

The "Archduke" Trio, Beethoven's last piano trio, was dedicated to his friend and patron the Archduke Rudolph of Austria. It does not always follow that last works are best, but in this case there can be no argument. At its heart is one of the most profound slow movements in the chamber music repertoire: a set of variations on a long-spanned, noble theme whose harmonic outline is more or less preserved while the melody is transformed almost beyond recognition before its eventual return in variation four, with its rich, romantic final scene.

4 Symphony No. 7 in A, Op. 92. Finale: Allegro con brio

After the music itself, the most famous thing about the Seventh Symphony (1812) is Wagner's characterization of it as "the apotheosis of the dance." Certainly no symphony thus far (and that includes the Fifth) is more rhythm-based than this one, in which each movement derives its greatest unity from the almost obsessive repetition and development of certain basic rhythmic patterns. This is also a symphony with no real slow movement. The nearest equivalent is the imposing introduction to the first movement, which was the most spacious ever written and which characteristically sows many of the seeds that come to fruition in the main part of the movement.

5 Mass in D, Op. 123 "Missa solemnis." Gloria: "Quoniam tu solus sanctus"

The *Missa solemnis* is such a profoundly symphonic, "organic" work, of such titanic proportions, that there are very few sections that can be cleanly extracted. Selected here is the final section, beginning with the words "Quoniam tu solus sanctus," of the massive Gloria. The Gloria as a whole falls into three parts. The first, "Gloria in excelsis Deo," is a hymn of praise to the "Lord God, Lamb of God, Son of the Father." The middle section, "Qui tollis peccata mundi," is a plea for mercy, and the third, presented here, affirms the uniqueness of the Holy Trinity: "Thou alone art Holy/Thou alone art the Lord/Thou alone art the Most High, Jesus Christ/With the Holy Spirit, in the glory of God the Father."

6 Piano Sonata No. 32 in C minor, Op. 111
Movement 2: Arietta. Adagio molto, semplice e cantabile

Beethoven's last three sonatas, Opp. 109–111, take us onto hallowed ground. Each creates a universe all its own, each defies meaningful description, taking us on a kind of spiritual space odyssey, into uncharted regions of the soul. The last sonata of all, Op. 111 in C minor, is a kind of celestial overview of his life's journey, from the fate-defying struggle and mastery reflecting the crisis of his mounting deafness to the simplicity and serenity found in the music of his final years. For many musicians and music lovers this is the greatest sonata ever written. The first movement is mighty, defiant, tightly controlled, propelled by an almost demonic intensity. The second (and last) movement, by contrast, is extraordinarily spacious, opening onto vast new horizons. Based on a theme of unsullied purity, the following variations are astonishingly wide-ranging (one bordering on ragtime and jazz), the surprises come thick and fast, and the air of spirituality lies beyond verbal description. This is perhaps the most transcendent Amen in the history of piano music.

[7] String Quartet in B flat, Op. 130. **Movement 5: Cavatina. Adagio molto espressivo**

After the intense and concise "Serioso" Quartet of 1810, as remarkable for its compression as the "Eroica" Symphony and the "Razumovsky" Quartets are for their revolutionary expansion, almost fifteen years passed before Beethoven returned to the medium. He then turned out five unique works. For many they constitute the greatest music ever written, regardless of medium or form. Even more than Op. 111, they carry us into new realms of spiritual experience. Each is the product of arguably the most powerful intellect in musical history, working at full stretch, and each requires absorbed and repeated attention. According to the violinist Karl Holz, who played in the premieres of the late quartets, the Cavatina fifth movement of Op. 130 "cost the composer tears in the writing and provoked the confession that nothing he had written had so moved him."

[8] Symphony No. 9 in D minor, Op. 125 "Choral." **Finale: Presto**

The Ninth Symphony would have secured an important place in history even without its groundbreaking choral finale (setting Schiller's *Ode to Joy*). Never had a symphony approached the proportions of this one. But while much was truly revolutionary, it can also be seen as the culmination of the eighteenth-century symphonic ideal. Beethoven still uses sonata form as the principal agent of dramatic movement; he still includes a scherzo (itself in sonata form); and he still uses the opposition and eventual reconciliation of different keys as a major structural and expressive device. But he does it all on such a huge canvas, and with such awe-inspiring emotional and intellectual power, that one easily feels like an eavesdropper at the Creation. Among its many unique features is the fact that the vast finale (a large part of which is heard here) contains within it not only the essential framework of Classical sonata form but that of an entire Classical symphony. More than any other Beethoven work, the Ninth Symphony opened the floodgates of high Romanticism.

Index

A

Æschylus, 120
Albrechtsberger, Johann Georg, 18, 178, 185
Arnold, Samuel, 151
Averdonk, Johanna Helena, 5

B

Bach, C.P.E., 36, 178
Bach, J.S., 6–7, 23, 37, 47, 69, 134, 140, 158, 172, 178, 186, 193
Balzac, Honoré de, 162, 164
Bartók, Béla, 177
Beethoven family,
- Caspar Carl van (brother), 8, 41–3, 45, 105
- Johann van (father), 4–5, 7–8, 18, 35, 110
- Johanna van (sister-in-law), 105–8, 112–13, 142, 147, 149, 154
- Karl van (nephew), 105–16, 133, 141–2, 146–9, 154, 189
- Ludwig Maria van (deceased brother), 4

- Ludwig van,
LIFE:
- and pianos, 5–6, 14, 33, 101, 116
- and the piano (as composer), 21–30, 35, 39, 40, 46–51, 64–6, 74, 89, 92, 96–8, 117, 120–1, 133, 159, 162, 179, 188, 197–203
- and the string quartet, 23, 47, 49, 51, 57, 133, 136–42
- and the symphony, v, 7, 21, 23, 27, 39, 40, 46, 54–5, 66–7, 76–7, 89–95, 102, 110, 117, 120–1, 133, 138–9, 144–5, 146, 155, 157–9, 163, 173, 198–200, 202–4
- annuities settled on, 34, 73, 100
- appearance of, 78, 109, 117, 150, 163
- as businessman, 10, 73
- as conductor, 61, 62–3, 144
- as organist, 7
- as pianist, 5, 10–14, 17, 19, 36, 61–2, 85, 104, 135
- as teacher, 36–8, 134
- as unofficial head of family, 8, 17
- as violinist/viola player, 5, 23, 47
- biographies of, 187
- character of, vii, 2–3, 5–6, 8–11, 14, 16–20, 22, 30, 32–3, 37–45, 54–63, 72–88, 100–117, 122, 126–134, 140–1, 144–7, 150–4
- childhood of, 2–8
- composing methods, 56, 85–6, 122, 128, 160
- concerts, 5, 34, 61
- conversation books, 109, 113
- deafness of, 29, 32–3, 35, 42, 45, 61, 76, 78, 85, 133, 144, 199, 203
- death and funeral of, 51, 144–5
- death of mother, 7
- depression, 10, 100, 150
- descriptions of, 19, 34–5, 40, 78, 101, 104, 117, 131, 141, 147, 151, 153–4
- earliest musical activities, 5–7
- eccentricity, viii, 35, 79, 88, 109, 117, 128
- education
  - in composition and theory, 5–6, 18
  - in piano and organ, 5
  - in violin and viola, 5
- extemporisation (see improvisations)
- finances of, 10, 34, 73, 100, 103, 152
- food and drink, tastes in, 117, 129, 132
- friendships, 3, 7–10, 14, 17–18, 20, 28, 32–3, 37, 40, 44, 59, 79, 109, 114, 117, 130–1, 145, 152–4, 184
- Haydn, relations with, 18, 151
- humor of, 20, 24, 28, 30, 95–6, 130, 139, 145–6, 185, 197, 200
- illnesses of, 32, 43, 78, 133, 141, 145, 148–50, 152–3
- improvisations by, 5, 7, 12–14, 26, 37, 61, 96, 104, 180
- in love, 39–40, 58–61, 78–83
- literary interests of, vii
- manners of, 14, 17, 19, 37, 78–9, 109, 119, 130, 137, 144
- marriage, thoughts of, 39, 58, 78, 83
- moral outlook of, vii, 10, 18, 77, 106
- nature, love of, 45, 81, 86
- operatic work, 66, 102, 119, 123–4
- patrons of, 16, 20, 27, 73, 119, 137, 181–4, 186
- philosophy, viii
- pianistic duels, 11–13
- political views of, vi–vii
- quarrels, 128, 147, 149
- relations with brothers, 42–3, 107, 113
- relations with father, 4–5, 7–8, 18, 110
- relations with mother, 9
- relations with royalty and aristocracy, 16–20, 27, 73, 100, 119, 137, 181–4, 186
- religion, views of, 2, 18, 69, 85, 154, 158
- reputation of, 10–11, 16–20, 35, 63, 72, 78, 117
- residences of, 81, 87, 101, 103, 112
- resilience of, 5, 78
- sense of humor (see humor)
- servants, 104, 106, 108, 112, 128
- sexual life of, 59–60, 76, 100
- social life in Vienna, 18, 20, 32, 145
- studies (see education)
- suicidal thoughts, 44–5
- tastes in dress, 34, 40, 109, 137, 151
- tastes in food, 132
- teachers of (see education)
- travels, 7, 9, 81, 84, 150
- women, relationships with, 19, 40, 58–60, 76, 79–83, 100, 122

MUSIC:
Adagio for three horns, 51
Adelaide, Song, Op. 46, 65
Ah! perfido, Scena and Aria, Op. 65, 61, 119
An die ferne Geliebte, Op. 98, 65

Bagatelles, Opp. 119 and 126, 40, 188
"Battle" Symphony, Op. 91, 67, 101–2, 183
Cantatas, 15, 64, 66–7, 189
Christus am Oelberge, Oratorio, Op. 85, 67
Consecration of the House, The, Overture, (see *Ruins of Athens, The*), 124, 133, 181–2
Concerto for piano, violin, cello and orchestra ("Triple Concerto"), Op. 56, 96, 98
Concerto for violin in D, Op. 61, 61, 96–7, 162, 201
Concertos, piano,
- No. 1 in C, Op. 15, 96, 120, 135
- No. 2 in B flat, Op. 19, 96, 120, 197
- No. 3 in C minor, Op. 37, 39, 96, 162
- No. 4 in G, Op. 58, 61–2, 92, 96, 201
- No. 5 in E flat, Op. 73 ("Emperor"), 75, 97
Contredanses, Twelve, WoO14, 120–1
Coriolan, Overture, Op. 62, 123, 162
Creatures of Prometheus, The, Ballet, Op. 43, 39, 120
Egmont, Overture and Incidental Music, Op. 84, 84, 123–4, 162
Equali for four trombones, WoO30, 51
Fantasia for piano, chorus and orchestra, ("Choral Fantasy"), Op. 80, 61, 67
Fidelio, Op. 72 (also *Leonore*), vi, 66, 103, 107, 119, 121–4, 162, 164, 200
King Stephen, Op. 117, 124, 182
Leonore Overtures Nos 1–3, 123
Mass in C, Op. 86, 61, 67
Mass in D, Op. 123 ("Missa solemnis"), 10, 67–8, 75, 117, 133, 180, 203
Missa solemnis, (see Mass in D), 10, 67–8, 75, 117, 133, 180, 203
National Airs with Variations, Opp. 105 and 107, 51
Octet in E flat, Op. 103, 48
Quartets, string, 39, 48, 57, 61, 100, 133, 136, 138–42
- in F, Op. 18 No. 1, 136
- in G, Op. 18 No. 2, 137
- in D, Op. 18 No. 3, 137
- in C minor, Op. 18 No. 4, 137
- in A, Op. 18 No. 5, 137
- in B flat, Op. 18 No. 6, 139
- in F, Op. 59 No. 1 ("Razumovsky"), 137–8
- in E minor, Op. 59 No. 2 ("Razumovsky"), 57, 137–8
- in C, Op. 59 No. 3 ("Razumovsky"), 137–8
- in E flat, Op. 74 ("Harp"), 139
- in F minor, Op. 95 ("Serioso"), 139
- in E flat, Op. 127, 139–40
- in B flat, Op. 130, 140–1
- in C sharp minor, Op. 131, 140
- in A minor, Op. 132, 140–1
- in B flat, Op. 133 ("Grosse Fuge"), 141
- in F, Op. 135, 141–2
Quintet in E flat for piano and wind, Op. 16, 49
Quintets, strings,
- in E flat, Op. 4, 136
- in C, Op. 29, 39
Ritterballett, WoO1, 186
Rondino in E flat, WoO25, 49
Ruins of Athens, The, Op. 113, 124, 182

Septet, E flat, Op. 20, 27, 34, 49–50
Serenade in D for violin and viola, Op. 25, 51
Sextet in E flat for two clarinets, two oboes, two horns, and two bassoons, Op. 71, 49
Sextet in E flat for two horns and string quartet, Op. 81b, 49
Sonatas, cello and piano,
- in F, Op. 5 No. 1, 47
- in G minor, Op. 5 No. 2, 47
- in A, Op. 69, 47
- in C, Op. 102 No. 1, 47
- in D, Op. 102 No. 2, 47
Sonata in F for horn and piano, Op. 17, 39, 51
Sonatas, piano,
- in F minor, Op. 2 No. 1, 21, 23
- in A, Op. 2 No. 2, 21, 23
- in C, Op. 2 No. 3, 21, 23
- in E flat, Op. 7, 24
- in C minor Op. 10 No. 1, 24
- in F, Op. 10 No. 2, 24
- in D, Op. 10 No. 3, 24
- in C minor, Op. 13 ("Pathétique"), 22, 24–6, 35, 38, 198
- in E, Op. 14 No. 1, 25
- in G, Op. 14 No. 2, 25
- in B flat, Op. 22, 25
- in A flat, Op. 26 ("Funeral March"), 25, 2, 39
- in E flat, Op. 27 No. 1 ("quasi una fantasia"), 25
- in C sharp minor, Op. 27 No. 2 ("quasi una fantasia," "Moonlight"), 25–7, 39–40, 199
- in D, Op. 28 ("Pastoral"), 26, 39
- in G, Op. 31 No. 1, 26
- in D minor, Op. 31 No. 2 ("Tempest"), 26, 40
- in E flat, Op. 31 No. 3, 26
- in G minor, Op. 49 No. 1, 26–7
- in G, Op. 49 No. 2, 26–7
- in C, Op. 53 ("Waldstein"), 26–7, 138, 186, 199
- in F, Op. 54, 27–8
- in F minor, Op. 57 ("Appassionata"), 22, 27–8, 33, 138, 199
- in E flat, Op. 81a ("Das Lebewohl" or "Les Adieux"), 28, 75
- in E minor Op. 90, 28
- in A, Op. 101, 28
- in B flat, Op. 106 ("Hammerklavier"), v, 24, 28–9, 47, 75, 126
- in E, Op. 109, 28–9
- in A flat, Op. 110, 28–9
- in C minor, Op. 111, 28–9
Sonatas, violin and piano,
- in D, Op. 12 No. 1, 47
- in E flat, Op. 12 No. 3, 47
- in A minor, Op. 23, 39
- in F, Op. 24 ("Spring"), 39
- in A, Op. 30 No. 1, 40
- in C minor, Op. 30 No. 2, 40
- in G, Op. 30 No. 3, 40
- in A, Op. 47 ("Kreutzer"), 48, 179, 182, 185
- in G, Op. 96, 84

Symphonies,
- No. 1 in C, Op. 21, 7, 39, 89–90, 120, 198
- No. 2 in D, Op. 36, 40, 54, 90–1, 158, 199–200
- No. 3 in E flat, Op. 55 ("Eroica"), v, 21, 27, 30, 54–6, 89–91, 93, 95, 121, 138–9, 158, 199, 204
- No. 4 in B flat, Op. 60, 91
- No. 5 in C minor, Op. 67, 61, 76, 89, 91–4, 162, 192, 202
- No. 6 in F, Op. 68 ("Pastoral"), v, 21, 61, 89–91, 93, 110
- No. 7 in A, Op. 92, 93–5, 103, 157, 202
- No. 8 in F, Op. 93, 94–5, 103
- No. 9 in D minor, Op. 125 ("Choral"), v, 21, 66–7, 89, 95, 117, 133, 144–5, 159, 204
Trio for two oboes and cor anglais, Op. 87, 51
Trios for piano, violin, and cello,
- in E flat, Op. 1 No. 1, 21, 23, 46, 182
- in G, Op. 1 No. 2, 21, 23, 46, 182
- in C minor, Op. 1 No. 3, 21, 23, 46, 182, 197–8
- in D, Op. 70 No. 1 ("Ghost"), 46
- in B flat, Op. 97 ("Archduke"), 47, 75, 202
- in B flat, WoO39, 178–9
Trios, string,
- in E flat, Op. 3, 49
- in G, Op. 9 No. 1, 136
- in D, Op. 9 No. 2, 136
- in C minor, Op. 9 No. 3, 136
Variations (miscellaneous),
- on Mozart's "Là ci darem la mano," in C for two oboes and cor anglais, WoO28, 51
Variations, piano,
- on an Original Theme in C minor, WoO80, 29
- on an Original Theme in F, Op. 34, 29, 38, 40
- on an Original Theme in E flat, Op. 35 ("Eroica"), 30, 40, 121
- on a Waltz by Diabelli, Op. 120, 29–30, 132, 178, 180
Wellingtons Sieg, Op. 91 (see "Battle" Symphony), 67, 101

Beethoven family (continued),
- Nickolaus Johann (brother), 8, 41, 147
- Maria Magdalena van (mother), 7, 9
- Therese (sister-in-law), 147
Berlioz, Hector, 94, 156–7, 162, 179
Blanchard, Henri-Louis, 162
Böhm, Josef, 144
Bonaparte, Napoleon, v–vii, 54–5, 66, 100–1, 167, 174, 199
Brahms, Johannes, 156, 177, 192
Breitkopf & Härtel (music publishers), 55
Brentano, Antonie, 79, 178
Brentano, Bettina, 178
Brentano, Maximiliane, 178
Bridgetower, George, 179
Bruckner, Anton, 158, 177
Bülow, Hans von, 23
Bunny, Bugs, 135
Bursy, Dr Karl von, 116

C
Cherubini, Maria Luigi, 161, 179
Chopin, Fryderyk, 156, 181–2, 192–3
Clement, Franz, 61
Clementi, Muzio, 179, 181
Collin, Heinrich von, 123
Cramer, Johann Baptist, 6, 179
Czerny, Carl, 7, 13, 29, 34, 36–7, 130, 134, 178–9, 181, 187

D
Dannhauser, Joseph, 163
Debussy, Claude, 176–7, 193
Deym, Countess Josephine (*née* Brunsvik), 58–61, 180
Diabelli, Anton, 180
Dressler, Ernst Christoph, 6
Duport, Jean-Pierre, 144

E
Elector Max Franz, of Bonn, 48
Ense, Karl von, 85
Ertmann, Baroness, 37
Esterházy, Prince Nikolaus, 68

F
Fétis, François-Joseph, 180

G
Galitsin, Prince Nikolas, 133, 145, 180
Gelinek, Abbé Josef, 11, 180
Gluck, Christoph Willibald, 19, 37, 173
Goethe, Johann Wolfgang von, vii, 67, 84–5, 123, 170, 176, 178, 181
Guicciardi, Countess Giulietta, 37, 39

H
Habeneck, François-Antoine, 161–2
Hähnel, Ernst, 163
Handel, George Frideric, 28, 37, 124, 140, 152, 156, 172–3, 186, 193
Hanon, Charles-Louis, 29
Haydn, Joseph, iv–v, viii, 6, 18–19, 21–2, 24, 46–8, 57, 64, 66–7, 72, 90–2, 136–7, 150–1, 156, 173, 176, 178, 182–3, 185–6, 189, 194, 198, 200
Hegel, G.W.F., 1
Heiligenstadt Testament, 41, 45, 54–5, 76
Hiller, Ferdinand von, 150–1, 181
Hoffmann, E.T.A., 176
Holz, Karl, 133, 145, 204
Homer, vii, 163
Hugo, Victor, 158, 164
Hummel, Johann Nepomuk, 150–1, 179, 181
Huneker, James, 159
Hüttenbrenner, Anselm, 154

I
Ives, Charles, 176–7

J

Jean-Christophe, 164
Jean Paul, 176
Josephstadt Theatre, Vienna, 124
Junker, Carl Ludwig, 10–12

K

Kant, Immanuel, viii, 169–70, 181
Kinsky, Prince Ferdinand, 73–4, 100, 180–1
Kotzebue, August von, 72, 158–9, 181
Kozeluch, Leopold, 66, 182
Kreutzer, Rodolphe, 182

L

Lamartine, Alphonse de, 158, 164
Lantz, Walter, 135
Lenz, Wilhelm von, 160, 182
Lichnowsky, Count Moritz von, 182
Lichnowsky family, 19
Lichnowsky, Prince Karl von, 19, 34, 44, 182
Liszt, Franz, 134–5, 156–7, 177, 179, 181–2
Lobkowitz, Prince Franz Joseph, 73–4, 100, 181, 183

M

Mahler, Gustav, 144, 158, 177
Malfatti, Dr Giovanni, 183
Malfatti, Therese, 78–9, 83, 183
Mälzel, Johann Nepomuk, 101, 183
Mendelssohn, Felix, 156, 169
Mona Lisa, 138
Moscheles, Ignaz, 35, 72, 149, 152–3
Mozart, Leopold, 5, 186
Mozart, Wolfgang Amadeus, v, vii, 5, 6–8, 12–13, 19, 21, 25–6, 36, 47–9, 56, 64–5, 72, 90–2, 96–7, 106, 121, 136–7, 155–6, 161, 171, 173, 179, 181–2, 184–6, 189, 191, 195, 197–8

N

Neefe, Christian Gottlob, 5–7, 183

O

Odescalchi, Princess, 37

P

Paganini, Nicolò, 97
Palestrina, Giovanni, 140
Picasso, Pablo, 135
Plato, 163
Pleyel, Ignaz Josef, 66, 182–3
Plutarch, vii, 77, 163

R

Radicati, Felice, 138
Razumovsky, Count Andrey, 57, 184
Reicha, Antonín, 14, 184
Rellstab, Ludwig, 39, 124
Ries, Ferdinand, 7, 19, 33, 38, 54–5, 109, 131, 134, 184
Rio, Giannatasio del, 107

Rolland, Romain, 164
Romeo and Juliet (Shakespeare), 124, 137
Rossini, Gioacchino, 133
Rudolph, Archduke, 20, 28, 68, 73–5, 100, 133, 181, 184, 202
Russell, Sir John, 117

S

Salieri, Antonio, 65, 119, 184
Schaden, Josef, 8
Schiller, Friedrich von, vii, 95, 155, 159, 170, 204
Schindler, Anton, 38, 76, 78, 86, 103, 108, 128, 132, 149–50, 153, 164, 184
Schmidt, Dr Johann, 43
Schoenberg, Arnold, 157–8, 160, 176
Schopenhauer, Arthur, 175
Schubert, Franz, 50, 56, 64–5, 154, 156, 158, 176–7, 190, 192
Schumann, Robert, 28, 65, 156, 90, 192
Schuppanzigh, Ignaz, 57, 138, 185
Scott, Sir Walter, viii, 150, 176
Seyfried, Ignaz Ritter von, 13, 61–2, 87, 103, 129–31, 185
Shakespeare, William, vii, 79, 123, 130, 137
Sibelius, Jan, 156
Simrock, Nicolaus, 185
Simpson, Robert, 156
Smart, Sir George, 152–3
Smetana, Bedrich, 33
Socrates, 158
Solomon, Maynard, 79, 187
Spohr, Louis, 61, 105, 159, 185
Steibelt, Daniel, 12, 185
Stravinsky, Igor, 177
Stumpff, Johann, 151–3
Swieten, Baron Gottfried van, 6, 184

T

Tannhäuser (Wagner), 156
Telemann, Georg Philipp, 48
Thomson, George, 66, 182, 186
Thun, Countess, 19
Tippett, Sir Michael, 156
Trémont, Baron de, 101
Troyer, Count Ferdinand, 50

V

Verdi, Giuseppe, 156
Vigano, Salvatore, 120
Vigny, Alfred de, 158, 164

W

Wagner, Richard, 7, 162, 175, 177, 186, 202

Acknowledgments

All *books are a team effort. This one would not have been possible without the tireless support of my editors Genevieve Helsby and Richard Wigmore, and my wife Deborah, all of whose combination of unwavering standards, imaginative suggestions and inspiring erudition has been both a pleasure and a privilege from the outset. And last, but very far from least, I am indebted to Klaus Heymann, founder and CEO of Naxos Records, who came up with the idea in the first place.*

About the Author

Jeremy Siepmann is an internationally acclaimed writer, musician, teacher, and broadcaster, and the editor of *Piano* magazine. He has contributed articles, reviews, and interviews to numerous journals and reference works (including *The New Statesman, The Musical Times, Gramophone, BBC Music Magazine*, and *The New Grove Dictionary of Music and Musicians*), some of them being reprinted in book form (Oxford University Press, Robson Books). His previous books include a widely praised biography of Chopin, two volumes on the history and literature of the piano, and biographies of Brahms and Beethoven.

www.jeremysiepmann.com